The Wine Doctor

The Wine Doctor

Wine for beginners from a Doctor of Nursing Practice and French Wine Scholar

By

Dr. Jesse V. McClain IV DNP, APRN, FWS

WSET Certified

French Wine Scholar

To request permissions, contact the publisher at: vannysvineyards@gmail.com

www.vannysvineyards.com

Paperback: ISBN: 979-8-9870045-0-0

Hardcover: ISBN: 979-8-9870045-1-7

eBook: ISBN: 979-8-9870045-2-4

Audiobook: ISBN: 979-8-9870045-3-1

Dedication

To the love of my life Kelsey – I could not do any of this without your love and support. You are the most amazing person in the world.

To my two gorgeous daughters Noel Holly and Winter Lumi. You two are my heart and soul. I love you girls so much and I am so proud of you.

The Wine Doctor

Wine for beginners from a Doctor of Nursing Practice and French Wine Scholar

Contents

Introduction

Whether you grew up around a vineyard or have little to no knowledge about wine, this book can function as a guide to assist you. This book is not an absolute. This book is not the 'Bible of Wine.' Rather, this book is to function as a guide to assist you on your wine journey. My journey in the wine industry literally started at a fruit stand. There is no reason that your journey could not be similar.

When I was growing up, my family drank very little to no alcohol, therefore, we never really had wine around the house. My parents hardly touched alcohol and therefore I did not have any knowledge of the stuff until much later in life. I presume many of you are quite similar, but I also realize that this is not always the case. My wife's family, contrarily, had wine with almost every dinner. She comes from a strong Italian background, and it was customary to have a bottle of red wine at the table with meals.

No matter your knowledge base, whether it be like mine growing up or my wife growing up, this book can help you understand the wines in our world today.

Wine has been around for thousands of years. In fact, the earliest mention of wine was 6000 BC. Within all the books of the Bible, wine is referenced 262 times. Throughout time, the industry of wine had its "booms" or advances, but it also suffered its depressions. The American wine industry was just beginning to thrive when, in 1920, it came to a crashing, almost abrupt halt. In 1920, Prohibition was implemented and alcohol as we knew it was banned, including wine. That is, unless it was earmarked as sacramental wine. Prohibition's 13-year reign made it very difficult for vineyards and vineyard owners. Almost four decades after Prohibition ended, the United States achieved the unachievable. David Conquered Goliath in a competition known as The Judgement of Paris. In 1976, the United States beat France in not only the white wine category but also the red wine category. At the time, little to no one knew the competition even took place. One lonesome reporter (George Taber) from *Time Magazine* showed up to cover the competition. The competition took place on May 24th, 1976, and the article was published in *Time Magazine* on June 7, 1976. The article was in the mid to back of the magazine (society section) and next to a car tire ad. Again, no one cared. But what that competition did for the wine industry not just in California, but America is not to be believed.

Those "kids from the sticks" as Jim Barrett (Chateau Montelena) put it, dominated French wine. This competition pitted California Chardonnay against some of the most well-respected White Bourgogne this world has ever known. It also put California Cabernet Sauvignon against the best of the best Bordeaux wines, including some First Growths.

The winner in the white wine category was the Chateau Montelena 1973 Chardonnay from California. The winner in the red wine category was the Stag's Leap Wine Cellars' 1973 Cabernet Sauvignon from California. Both wins were tremendous upsets and to this day, the best thing to happen to the American wine industry – in my opinion. (Well, many experts' opinion)

Though this book is not designed to educate you about the history of wine, I did design it to give you little snippets of information. Information that I hope you find useful as you are looking to educate and train your own palate. This book is for both novices as well as experts. For example, I will touch on a few facts about the grapes themselves but also tell you about the inside-joke that even the biggest wine expert probably missed. No matter your skill level, there is something for everyone.

This book will teach you how to taste wine like how you taste a pizza. The pizza/wine comparison is a no-miss when it comes to identifying what you like and what you do not like when it comes to wine. It is how I taste wine and is just one way to "skin a cat" per se, but if done properly can be quite useful. I use this comparison in all my wine talks.

Many chapters in this book provide knowledge in one facet of the industry, from the grapes themselves to the size of the bottle used to store the wine. I attempt to teach anyone and everyone the same way whether it be in one of my live wine classroom sessions or in this text. I will teach you the appropriate way to taste wine. For it is my belief, if wine is tasted the same way each time, identifying the wine with or without the label becomes a lot easier.

The layout of this book is slightly different than your standard "Beginner's Guide." Rather, I designed this book to be filled with nuggets or tidbits to help you have a "leg-up" on those in the same room tasting the same wine. How? Well, yes, I am going to tell you about the a few grapes, but instead of explaining the flavor profile you should expect from say, Cabernet, I will provide you bullet-point facts about the grape and/or the vine. This will increase your knowledge and make dinner conversation a little more interesting because most of the bullet points explained in each section are not widely known by even some of the so-called experts.

Dispersed amongst the chapters, I will also impart some medical/ knowledge regarding wine. Given my medical background I would be remiss if I did not guide you along that path as well. I originally planned a health chapter but decided instead to disperse the health aspects of wine throughout the book, for this book is written by The Wine Doctor, is it not?

But first, allow me to provide a little background as to who I am and why I do what I do.

One
The Wine Business

For much of my professional career things just seemed to happen to me. As bizarre as it may sound, I never interviewed for any job I ever held. EVER. Sure, I interviewed for a couple jobs growing up; two in fact. Interestingly, I never was offered either. The two companies I interviewed with Toys R' Us and Old Navy and both were when I was in high school. Interestingly, neither manager ever called me back for a job or even a second interview. Maybe I just do not interview well.

When I was in high school, I was certain I wanted to work in film. I did not necessarily think I wanted to be a movie star, though my family always felt I was a good actor. Instead, I wanted to be behind the scenes, such as a director or even work in audio of some sort. I was always fascinated with the film industry and as early as middle school I was part of the first group of students to run the school's television network. In fact, it quite possibly was the first group in the state or country to run a student television network. The year was 1990/1991. I was the audio engineer for our morning news program which provided updates for what was going on within the school system. 6th grade and I was the audio engineer? For sure, this was my chosen career path. Right?

Wrong. While I was still in high school, I was enrolled in the local University. Yes, I was one of those people, but only because my father was a teacher and knew the state offered such a program. The benefit was essentially a "free" year of college, but the downside was I became ineligible for my senior year of tennis (which was ok).

Youngstown State University (YSU) was close and was a very exciting University at the time. Our football program essentially played in the National Championship game every year in the 1990s. Think Alabama (at the time of writing this book) but in the One double A level. It was so fun, and the head coach was the dad of a friend from middle school. While I attended YSU, I was able to secure a job in the athletic training room covering football and eventually earned myself a National Championship ring as well as a "Team of the Decade" ring without being hit one time. Genius, right?!

My career goals then pivoted from audio engineer to a professional athletic trainer. Unfortunately, at the time of my attendance, YSU did not offer such a major and I was not too keen on transferring to a different school. I then pivoted my major to "pre-nursing" and the rest is history, sort of. I eventually was accepted into the program and made several friends, many of which I still talk to today. One friend was being hired at a local hospital after graduation and convinced me to accompany him to fill out paperwork before we grabbed a quick bite to eat. At that time, I honestly had no clue what I was going to do when I graduated but as fate would have it, I started talking to another hospital manager while I waited for my friend. Before I knew it, I was hired and working steady midnights in the Medical Intensive Care Unit. Again, no formal interview.

Shortly after I started, I realized I was not going to be able to do this for 40+ years. There were many nurses who were 60+ and still working in the ICU and when I did the math, I was terrified. A new friend from the ICU convinced me to go back to school with her so I did. "Misery loves company" was the phrase I distinctly recall. I was on track to get my Master's in Nursing but had no idea what I then wanted to do for a living upon graduation.

Part of the master's program involved clinical rotations with physicians or other master's prepared nurses. Advanced Practice Nurses were essentially not that popular yet so there were very few that I could find to do rotations with. Hardly any at all in fact. I found one who was practicing in neurology and asked if I may join her for a few hours. She obliged and the neurology practice where she worked offered me a job after I graduated. I have been working in that practice since 2006. Again, no formal interview.

My fascination with wine

I purchased my first home in 2005. A small, 1200 square foot condo just south of Youngstown. I did not have a basement, but I did have a temperature-controlled garage. One fall, I was driving down the road, home form the hospital when I came across a fruit stand advertising the fact they had "White Niagara, great for winemaking" grapes for sale. Never having heard of these grapes and intrigued by the process of making wine, I felt compelled to stop and check it out. They had crates full of this greenish grape with a sign that said, great for winemaking. So, I thought I would give it a go.

Well, I read all that I could; magazine articles, chapters in books (the internet was not that useful in 2007/2008) for things such as this. I also talked to several people at the hospital who dabbled in the making of "hooch." My first batch was terribly cloudy. Nevertheless, I decided to enter the Canfield Fair. This was a local county fair (though the biggest in Ohio), but I presumed it would be good to receive some "professional" feedback.

Personally, I felt my wine was awful. But, somehow, I garnered a pink ribbon, which meant "honorable mention." To this day, I still believe they give all first-time entries an honorable mention ribbon to keep them coming back and re-entering, year after year. My second and third year were equally awful but never garnered any critical acclaim.

To learn my faults (what I was doing wrong), I decided to enroll in the American Wine Academy and officially study wine. I wanted to know what made wine "good" and what made wine bad. My first class was amazing – "Wine 101" Remember, I did not grow up with wine, so I honestly had no clue as to what made a wine good or bad. This was an eye-opening experience.

While I was there, I asked about the series of courses which allowed a person to sit for international certification once completed. I enrolled in the Wine Spirits Education and Trust coursework and began studying immediately. Throughout my coursework, there were numerous volunteer opportunities in Cleveland to assist me in learning certain skills related to drinking and serving wine. One such opportunity was working a food show in Cleveland. It was this volunteer experience that introduced me to Guy Fieri and Curtis Stone from the Food Network. Guy, in fact, called me "the wine guy" that night – awesome.

I studied hard and eventually passed my certification exam. I began working for a chocolate company on the side from my daytime neurology practice. I would speak at wine tastes and would travel to fancy food shows selling the chocolate that was specifically designed to be paired with certain wines.

In my spare time, I would volunteer and host the annual Lions Club member engagement party. They would have new members and current members come out to eat and learn about wine with the idea of enticing new individuals to join their group. It was such a nice event, I enjoyed hosting it 8 years in a row. To this day, I still miss them.

I always considered pursuing my wine education further, but family and work commitments limited my ability to study abroad. Then SARS CoV-2 hit our country/world, and everyone was "locked down." As every college, high school, and even elementary school transitioned to remote learning styles, I thought to myself, 'I wonder if wine education world also made the pivot?' Well, I was correct, they did and in the late summer/early fall of 2020 I enrolled in the Wine Scholars Guild's French Wine Scholar program. For over a year, I participated in live lectures and asynchronous learning modules. I watched videos, read books, and took practice quizzes to become a French Wine Scholar. In 2021, I passed my certification exam with honors, all from the comfort of my wine cellar.

Throughout my wine education journey, I continued to make wine. Some wine I felt was good and some I felt was not so good. In 2020, I decided to make a Sauvignon Blanc. This was my first year at using a filter. If you are anywhere around the winemaking community, wine filtration seems to be a very polarizing technique in winemaking. People seem to either embrace it or vehemently abstain from using this technique. I always felt this was an unnatural way to make homemade wine, but after years of trying to clear white wine using more natural methods, I felt it was worth a try.

Wine filtration, as one of my friends stated, is like dialysis for winemaking. You literally suck the wine from one vat, send it through a filter and deposit the clearer wine into another vat. The process is quite remarkable and easy. The specific filter I used has 3 filtration options depending on how clear or free of particles you seek to achieve. I cleared it and then "polished" it with an extra fine filtration pad and let me tell you, the results were astounding. I made my white wine so crystal clear, and the flavor seemed to be unchanged.

Now, the true reason I decided to filter my wine in 2020 was because of feedback I received the year prior. In 2019, I decided to move on from the local county fair wine competition and submit my wine into an international competition. In 2019, I did not do well. Personally, I felt I over-oaked the wine and to me it tasted like wood. I received the three judges' feedback, and their scorecards were very telling. Their scorecards were essentially divided into three categories.

- Appearance
- Aroma
- Taste

Please see Appendix A for the actual scorecards from 2020 competition (2019's vintage).

As I reviewed the notes from the three judges, I realized one thing. Most of the issues I had no control over. But I did control how my wine looked. I may not have any control over the aroma or taste of the wine, but I could make it look gorgeous even if it tasted like trash. I mean, let's be honest; for sure I can ruin the flavor by leaving it in oak too long or adding to many chemicals/acids. I could improve the wine by altering a few things. However, I had no control over the flavor of the juice I purchased from France/Italy or wherever it came from that year. So, for the next year, I decided to focus on the thing I could control, The Look of my wine. I wanted to make the prettiest wine possible. Hence, my investment into a wine filtration system.

Psychology textbooks discuss the halo effect. The Halo Effect is essentially where one person's trait will alter your perception of the others. For example, if a guy is handsome, women may automatically presume he is also smart or ambitious. I felt this same effect applied to wine. If my wine looked amazing, then maybe the judges will in turn think it tasted amazing?

Maybe?

At any rate, I decided to filter the 2020 batch in hopes of getting a great score in the "appearance" category while also improving my "taste" category score.

Whatever happened at the competition, I do not know, but I can say that my changes helped. We scored well and earned enough points for a silver medal for our 2020 Sauvignon Blanc.

Please see Appendix B for the 2021 scorecards

I will leave it up to you all to decide, did my theory work about the look and taste of wine? Was it the Halo Effect at play during the competition? Who knows for certain? But I am absolutely sticking by that theory for now.

I chose to filter my 2021 Malbec as well. At the time of writing this chapter, the competition did not take place yet and I am anxiously awaiting the findings. Much against my previous stern belief, I chose to filter the 2021 Malbec. Yes, I chose to strip much of the perceived characteristics away just to score well on "look" category of the competition. This wine is crystal clear for a dark red. There is absolutely no sediment. There is no haze. It is a perfect deep garnet color and, per my belief, will also taste fresh, clean, and hopefully outstanding. All purely based off the Halo Effect. I also chose to not oak this wine. I wanted the cherry/raspberry and licorice flavor profiles to come through. I also had concerns about where my oak sticks were coming from if the judge from the 2019 competition felt it tasted like "mud." (However, from Appendix A's scorecard, judge number 11 gave me a 2 out of 3 for this "mud" flavor. A 2/3 quantifies a "good" score. So, am I safe to assume this means judge number 11 enjoys drinking mud?)

Travelling along this journey has been an experience. Long since I started making wine, I, at first, jokingly called my winery "Vanny's Vineyards." My middle name is VanDevner (yes, VanDevner) and my nickname was Vanny (to some). As a kid, I would be embarrassed or offended if someone made fun of it, but as an adult, I leaned into it and embraced it. In fact, my wife and I planned on naming our son VanDevner, but we ended up having two gorgeous daughters.

I appreciated the alliteration as well. I thought Vanny's Vineyards rolled off the tongue easily and the wine labels looked spectacular that I personally designed.

Now, that all being said, as the expenses grew and more people wanted to pay me for my product, I decided I better trademark the name and company. It also helps come tax time. However, I did not expect another person/business to use "Vanny," but I suppose you never know. I also thought, well, if this takes off like I hope it does, I am going to be very disappointed I did not trademark the name earlier. So, that is exactly what I did. I registered the name with the state of Ohio and officially started Vanny's Vineyards.

I always enjoyed writing, so the bulk of the vineyard's work is in wine education while also making award-winning wine. In 2022, I built the website, started a blog, and started the clothing line while also working on this book. I am excited to see what the future has in store for Vanny's Vineyards. Thank you for being a part of this journey.

Two
The Grapes

A grape used in winemaking is also known as a varietal.

In many countries, wines are given fancy names. Sometimes, the fancy name or pretty wine label is merely a marketing tool. It is quite common for wineries to also list the varietal or, what type of grape the bottle contains.

Unfortunately, this is not always the case – almost all the wines from France are labelled by region as opposed to grape variety and it is the wine buyer's responsibility to understand what grapes are permitted, by law, in the bottle. For this specific reason, people are intimidated when shopping for wine and/or avoid many sections of the wine store. We will discuss how to navigate your local grocer or wine shop in the next chapter, but for now, let's focus on the varietals.

This chapter is about the grape or as previously stated, the varietal. Now, some literature reports that there are over 10,000 grapes in this world but for the purpose of this book, I will cover only a handful because, let's be honest, many of us will only taste a handful and not all 10,000. I will also not bore you with useless paragraph dialect, but rather, I am truly "just" going to give you bullet points on each grape I mention. This chapter essentially has only snippets of information for the newbie to survive in the wild. Whether it be shopping in a store or having a conversation with friends and family over dinner, these bullet points should set you a part regarding your newfound wine knowledge.

Sauvignon Blanc

1. This varietal comes from a region in France known as Bordeaux. Yes, that Bordeaux. It comes from the French words "sauvage" for wild and "blanc" for white.

2. Fume Blanc is nothing more than the varietal, Sauvignon Blanc. In the French region of Pouilly-Fume, their wine is known for their flinty notes found in their Sauvignon Blanc. Some from The New World in California thought it would be chic to give Sauvignon Blanc's name a spin and therefore dubbed it, Fume Blanc.

3. Sauvignon Blanc is the mother to Cabernet Sauvignon. That's right, Cabernet Sauvignon is a varietal that was a cross between Sauvignon Blanc and Cabernet Franc. When those two vines crossed together, they created Sauvignon Blanc.

4. Methoxypyrazines – say what??? This chemical compound is found in Sauvignon Blanc and tends, at times, to give off an herby type of nose/flavor. Many, tend to describe this sensory experience to be akin to cat pee or bell pepper. Yes, I said cat pee.

5. Regions known for Sauvignon Blanc, include the Marlborough region in New Zealand, many regions of California, Loire/Sancerre region in France and the sweet wines of Bordeaux in France. Yes, Bordeaux loves its sweet WHITE wines.

6. Common notes found in Sauvignon Blanc include, lemons, pears, fresh-cut grass, green bell pepper (from the pyrazine which will also be discussed further in Cabernet Sauvignon).

7. The first Friday in May is known as International Sauvignon Blanc Day.

Chardonnay

1. Originally from Bourgogne in France. Commonly referred to as "white Burgundy" but the wine community is attempting to steer away from the word Burgundy because the region is in fact called Bourgogne. More Chardonnay is planted in Bourgogne than Pinot Noir.

2. Malolactic Fermentation – Chardonnay gets much of its "smoothness" or buttery texture from a process called malolactic fermentation – NOT Oak. Though many Chardonnays are in fact "oaked." This process of fermentation occurs when the malic acid is converted to lactic acid (typically found in milk) which provides the smooth, buttery character many have come to know and love.

3. Not all Chardonnay is Oaked. Many in California are utilizing a style commonly used in the Bourgogne region of Chablis. They are aging their Chardonnays in Stainless Steel Vast as opposed to aging in oak which has been the standard for years.

4. Chardonnay is one of the main grapes found in Champagne. In fact, it is the only white grape found in Champagne. If the Champagne says Blanc de Blanc (white from white), then it is only made from Chardonnay.

5. Chardonnay gained much of its fame from Charlamagne who ordered this grape to be planted in Bourgogne because she was fed up with the Pinot Noir staining her husband's beard.

6. In 1976, Chateau Montelena's 1973 Chardonnay won the white wine competition in the Judgement of Paris: beating out many of the French's critically acclaimed whites from Bourgogne.

7. Chardonnay is the best-selling wine in America.

Cabernet Sauvignon

1. Stag's Leap 1973 Cabernet Sauvignon won in the red wine category during the 1976's Judgement of Paris beating out some of Bordeaux's greatest wine producers.

2. Cabernet Sauvignon is the offspring of Sauvignon Blanc and Cabernet Franc.

3. Pyrazine – as mentioned in the section about Sauvignon Blanc (Cabernet Sauvignon's mother). Methoxypyrazine is a chemical compound found in Cabernet Sauvignon and most wine tasting professionals look for this when blind tasting wines. If detected, the wine is easily identified in a blind-wine tasting. How? Well, this specific chemical compound is responsible for the flavor profile of a bell pepper. Therefore, this is the bouquet many detect in Cabernet Sauvignons or Sauvignon Blancs.

4. Most widely planted grape in the world and demand continues to rise.

5. Because of its thicker skin and high tannins, Cabernet Sauvignon is typically used as a blending agent. Cabernet Sauvignon is often blended with Merlot like salt is with pepper to make it more palatable or drinkable with less aging requirements.

6. Cabernet Sauvignon is the dominant grape on the left bank in Bordeaux and the focus of the upper echelon when it comes to wine. The grape that became the focus of the 1976 Paris Wine tasting competition with France and the United States.

Merlot

1. Though Cabernet Sauvignon is the most widely planted grape in the world, it is Merlot that is the most widely planted grape in Bordeaux. Yes, Merlot. Surprising, I know.

2. Merlot is found in every region of Bordeaux, but it most dominant on the right bank of the Gironde estuary in regions such as St. Emilion and Pomerol

3. Chateau Petrus is the most coveted wine in the world is almost entirely made from Merlot. This vineyard is located on the right bank of the Gironde Estuary.

4. **The world witnessed California's Merlot production drop** almost 21% in 2005/2006 **following the release of the movie** *Sideways*.

5. Merlot is quite sensitive to light and oxidizes easily. Therefore, you may quickly notice it turn a light shade of orange around the rim of your wine glass if sitting for a period.

6. Merlot is very food friendly and can be quite versatile when pairing it. This is because the grape, Merlot, the grape, tends to be higher in sugar and low in acidity. (This does not mean the wine is high in sugar or that it's a sweet wine.

Pinot Noir

1. Pinot Noir got its name over a thousand years ago because it looked like a black pinecone on the vine.

    a. "Noir" – French for Black

    b. "Pinot" – French for Pine.

2. Pinot Noir is a very finicky rape to grow and make wine from. This is for many reasons. One being that the grapes clusters are very tight and grow in clumps. This makes the space between the grapes very warm, and condensation does not evaporate easily making it quite suspectable to disease and rot. Another factor that makes it tough to grow is the fact it has a very thin outer coat (skin). This thin skin makes it easy for insects or other pests to penetrate therefore having easy access to all the good juice inside. This, in turn, leaves us nothing to make wine with.

3. In Bourgogne, their slopes dictate who the wine was intended for. The upper part of the slopes of Bourgogne were earmarked for the Cardinals in the Catholic church. The middle slope in Bourgogne was designated for the Pope himself. The lower part of the slope was for the bishop and the plains were for everyone else. These designations still hold some truth today but are not necessarily earmarked for the higher-ups of the Catholic church. For example, the middle part of the slope, once intended for the Pope now carries the designation of "Grand Cru" whereas the top of the slope, again, once intended for the Cardinals now carries the designation of "Premier Cru."

4. In 2005/2006 Pinot Noir production in California increased 170% because of the release of the critically acclaimed movie *Sideways.*

5. Pinot Noir is a grape utilized in the making of Champagne.

Syrah/Shiraz

1. Initially from the Rhone region in France. Typically blended with Grenache and Mourvèdre. Therefore, it is not uncommon for one to identify this blend as a "GSM." (Grenache, Syrah and Mourvèdre).

2. This grape is also known for its growth in Australia. However, in Australia, it is known as Shiraz. It is the same grape but just a slightly different name.

3. Though also a very similar name, Petit Syrah should not be compared to Syrah. It is a completely different grape variety that comes from a cross between Syrah and a varietal known as Peloursin.

4. Famously identified with appellations such as Cote Rotie in the Rhone region as well as Hermitage in the Rhone region.

5. Typically known for its spicy/peppery notes, Syrah makes some of the deepest, darkest red wines in the world.

Zinfandel

1. For years believed to be originally from America. It was recently proven to be the same grape variety as Italy's Primitivo and Croatia's Tribidrag.

2. Most people feel compelled to identify Zinfandel as the "Red Zinfandel" merely because of White Zinfandel's popularity. But, in fact, it is just Zinfandel. (Just a small gripe)

3. White Zinfandel was invented by Sutter Home in the early 1970s. originally made as a vineyard, tasting room exclusive wine. It was given a French sounding name (Oeil de Perdrix) but because of American wine law had to identify what the varietal was. Therefore, the label said, "White Zinfandel." This was originally some free-run juice that was barrel aged and sold. In one specific year, the fermentation process became stuck therefore leaving residual sugar behind which accidentally produced the sweeter wine many enjoy today.

4. By the mid 1980s, White Zinfandel was America's most popular wine.

Pinot Gris / Pinot Grigio

1. Originates in the Alsace region of France – where it is known as Pinot Gris

2. Pinot Grigio is a bluish-grey grape on the vine. It grows in clusters that tends to resemble a pinecone. This, in fact, is how it obtained its name.

   a. "Gris" – French for Grey

   b. "Pinot" – French for Pine.

3. One of the most popular wine styles from Italy – sometimes dubbed as "Cougar Juice" within the restaurant community. This implies that older women enjoy ordering Pinot Grigio. It is crisp, it is sweet, and it can be refreshing.

4. Depending on where it is grown, you may or may not like it – cooler regions tend to be sweeter than warmer regions.

   a. Alsace's versions tend to be sweeter whereas Californian and Italian versions tend to be more acidic and drier.

5. Probably the most perfect cooking wine – Chardonnay tends to be oaky or woody and Rieslings tend to be too sweet at times. Therefore, making Pinot Gris/Grigio to be perfect for your fish or pasta dishes.

Riesling

1. Like its cousin, Pinot Gris, Riesling also hales from the Alsace region in France. However, it has gained its notoriety or popularity in Germany which at many times occupied the region of Alsace.

2. Riesling is found in many countries but its most notably from Alsace, France and Mosel, Germany.

3. Though known to be a sweet wine, Alsace and Mosel are notorious for making some of the best Rieslings in the world and they are typically DRY.

4. "Late-Harvest" Riesling is a dessert wine made by allowing the grapes to stay on the vine longer and delay harvest. This delay allows a fungus (Botrytis cinerea) to dehydrate the grape causing it to be sweeter than if harvested at "normal" times.

5. By allowing Riesling to freeze on the vine before harvest, this then produces Ice Wine or Eiswein.

Three
Tasting Wine

As I previously mentioned, I am from Youngstown, Ohio. Over the decades, you may have heard several stories about our town. Some stories are somewhat true, and some stories are without a doubt true. But one thing for certain is that we have amazing pizza. Whether you like New York style or thicker crust style, we have a pie for you. During many of my wine talks, I find myself comparing tasting wine to tasting Youngstown pizza because this is something everybody in town can relate to and can appreciate. There is not a week that goes by that I am not faced with the same question.

"Can you really tell the difference between a $10 bottle of wine and a $200 bottle of wine?"

And I typically answer this question the same way -- and to my fellow Youngstowners, it makes complete sense. And, that response is ...

"Can you tell the difference between Wedgewood Pizza and Little Caesars?"

And almost every time I bite back with that question, they nod in approval. The nod is almost as if the person from Youngstown now completely gets me. As if they are saying "absolutely I can tell the difference between Wedgewood and Little Caesars."

Allow me to explain.

We all know the specific toppings we prefer on our pizza. This chapter is not designed to argue about whether pineapple belongs on pizza. Though, my opinion is that it absolutely does belong on pizza. Instead, it is to help you understand the styles of wine you like and do not like.

When you order pizza, where do you like to order pizza from?

Why do you like that pizza?

Is it their dough?

Is it their sauce?

Is it their cheese?

Is your favorite pizza shop one that puts way too much gritty crumbles (cornstarch) on the bottom of their pie?

Does your favorite pizza shop have a gigantic picture of its owner on the wall?

Do you prefer deep dish or thin style? Do you prefer a square slice or a triangle-shaped slice?

Being from eastern Ohio, do you prefer cold cheese topping on your pizza (look up Ohio Valley Pizza), or do you prefer melted cheese?

Whatever your preference is, you know what you like and what you do not like. You know which pizza you are in the mood for that day and which pizza you are not. "Oh, I cannot handle Avalon Gardens tonight because the dough is too heavy, can we get Bella Napoli, their cheese is amazing, and their dough is much thinner?"

Wine can and should be no different.

Why do we complicate how we drink wine but simplify how we eat a cheeseburger or pizza? Do you not prefer certain establishments when it comes to cheeseburgers as well? I believe it to be perfectly reasonable to appreciate regions in the world where you like Pinot Noir and regions you do not. I certainly have my preferences. Now, this by no means is saying you will never get pizza from those other places you do not prefer. It also means you will not drink wine made from grapes you do not prefer or regions you are not a fan of.

Tasting wine should be no different than tasting pizza. You typically taste pizza the same way – take the same bite – eat the same crust over and over. Do you fold your slice? Do you bite the pointy wedge off first? When it comes to square pieces do you like the corners, the squares with some crust or do you like the soggy, soft center with no crusty edge?

I encourage you to taste wine the same way each time. Sure, there may be days where you are so hungry you are not sure you even tasted the pizza just as there will be days you are not sure you ever tasted the wine. But, if you, most of the time, taste wine the same way and with the same method, sooner or later you will find your preferences. You will know the regions you like and the grapes you love.

For example, I like but do not love Pinot Noir. I like it from Oregon but not typically from California. And even though I am a French Wine Scholar, I am "so so" on the Pinot Noir from France. Yes, that includes the famed Bourgogne region. But how can that be? Isn't Pinot Noir the same in every state or every country? I taste my wine the same way every time and I found I like the cooler region and flavor profile of Oregon's Pinot Noir over California's Pinot Noir. Maybe the warmer climate dampens the fruit flavor for me when drinking Pinot noir?

Now, after all that, my absolute favorite Pinot Noir is Bloom's Field from Santa Barbara County, California. What sense does that make? Well, my statements are generalizations and not specific or absolute. Taste each wine individually. Just because I am not a fan of Chicago style pizza does not mean I do not like pizza in Chicago. I love me a Giordano's but overwhelmingly will not choose a deep-dish pizza if given an option. Unless Giordano's is in the mix. Same with Pinot Noir. I overwhelmingly will choose Oregon's Pinot Noir over Californian Pinot Noir unless Bloom's Field is an option. Just as Giordano's would be my choice, Bloom's Field would be my choice.

I hope this all makes a little sense.

The goal of this chapter is essentially to give you some bullet points on how to systematically taste wine. A "guide" per se as to what to look for and how to do it. I will explain how to look at wine, how to smell the wine and how to taste the wine as compared to eating, tasting pizza. I will also discuss how to come to your own conclusion about the wine you have tasted. If you follow these steps, over time, they will become second nature and tasting wine will be like tasting pizza. Shopping and selecting wine will then become quite easy. You find yourself comfortable with scouring the Pinot Noir section. Or you will find yourself asking the employee "can you point me to your Willamette Valley Pinot Noir section?"

How to look at wine

Is the wine red or white seems too easy? But rather ask yourself if it is light red, pale red, ruby, or even dark garnet. This will tell you a lot about the wine. To aid in identifying the color, hold the glass at an angle and place something white behind it. Typically, a white napkin or tablecloth would be ideal. During wine tastings, you will see white tablecloths or even white placemats to help the taster identify the true pigment of the wine.

Is it darker in the middle where the bulk of the wine sits?

What color do you see along the rim of the glass where the wine thins out?

In both red and white wines, as the wine ages, the rim will turn a hint of orange.

The intensity of the red wine also can tell you a lot about the grape without even looking at the wine label. The lighter red colors tend to be your thinner-skinned grape. Therefore, when you see a lighter red wine, the possibilities could be along the lines of a Zinfandel, Pinot Noir or possibly a Gamay. Your medium red intensity wines could be Merlot, or a Sangiovese and your darker red, almost purple hued wines could be Cabernet, Shiraz, or Malbec. Certainly, there are other possibilities (especially since there are over 10,000 varieties of wine) but these are some of the more common wines you will encounter.

Contrary to popular belief, legs of the wine DO NOT determine a wine's quality. Legs, also known as "tears," are present when you swirl a wine in your glass and watch how quick or slow the wine trickles along the side of the glass from the rim back down into the base of the glass. Legs are present because of a chemical reaction in the wine. The higher the alcohol content, the thicker or slower the legs. The lower the alcohol content the thinner or quicker the legs. The legs of a wine merely indicates a wine's alcohol content and NOT its quality or rating.

White wines tend to display either a silverish hue, lemon-yellow hue, or a deep gold almost thick yellow hue. The more silver looking wines tend to be extremely young and were most likely aged in stainless steel as opposed to oak. (Think silver and steel.) The more yellow (almost green) looking wines could be Sauvignon Blanc and the more golden white wines most likely were exposed to oak aging. This golden color most likely occurred from micro-oxygenation which occurs in the oak barrels. Stainless steel vats tend to not permit micro-oxygenation therefore do not have this greenish, yellow hue.

By identifying the color, its specific nature and the wine's viscosity will tell you more about the wine than you expect. By just looking at the glass you can already attest to its age, its alcohol content and possibly the wine's acidity. The more you identify the wine's little nuances by just looking at it through the same lens, you may already develop an opinion about it just as you would by opening a pizza box. The box may not give you any identifying markers (many mom-and-pop pizza shops use standard, cookie-cutter pizza boxes) but as soon as you open the box and look at the pie, you will formulate an opinion. Wine should be no different.

So, the next time you are poured a glass of wine, I want you to look at it for a few minutes before taking a sip.

- What do you see?
- Is it a red or white wine?
- Is it pale or deep in color?
- What does the rim color look like?
- Is it a younger or older wine?
- Are the legs thick or thin?
- Can you guess the alcohol percentage?
- Can you guess the grape?
- Does the hue make you think of a thin-skinned grape or a thicker-skinned grape?
- Does the color indicate if it was aged in stainless steel or oak?

And yes, you can absolutely answer all the above without even smelling or even tasting the wine.

How to smell wine

Sure, many wine drinkers are laughed at for what I am about to explain, but first and foremost, learn how to swirl a glass. Practice it. Swirl water repeatedly. The more you swirl a wine, the more you open it up. By doing this, you will not appear pretentious, to most.

Why is swirling so important?

Well, that wine has been bottled-up for who knows how long. Swirling the wine allows oxygen to come into contact with the wine which releases aroma compounds into the air. By not "waking" the wine up, these compounds will not be released, and the wine may have little to no aroma. Therefore, it may seem "tight." Sure, if you give it time, oxygen will do its thing (like and half eaten apple on your counter). But who wants to wait? Swirl it well and take a sniff.

Now, that initial sniff will shock your senses because your nose was not prepared. Your eyes were prepared because you spent a few minutes beforehand inspecting the color, hue, legs, etc. But your nose was not prepared. So, that initial "sniff" is a throw away. It does not count. That first sniff's sole purpose is merely to prepare the nose.

Think of a dog. How does a dog smell you? How does a dog smell a steak? Does he take one big whiff of the steak and walk away? No, that dog does not. Instead, he takes multiple little sniffs over and over while walking around the piece of meat. So, the next time you smell a wine, take a few smaller sniffs before committing your nose to the glass and start identifying specific scents.

When you do start identifying specific scents, I always want you to identify three. But I want those three to be something everyone can relate to. For example, saying a wine reminds you of your grandmother's kitchen tells us nothing. Unless the people at your table know your grandmother, making a statement like that is unrelatable. It means nothing. Saying it reminds you of oregano, says a lot more to everyone at the table. We all know what Oregano smells like. We have no clue what your grandmother's kitchen smelled like because mine smelled of smoke; therefore, I cannot relate to your grandmother's garlic smelling kitchen. The three scents you identify should be easily translatable across the table. I always want you to identify three, but this will take some time and is intended to make you think; maybe even overthink.

Sometimes, you may encounter a faulty wine. A faulty wine is a wine that has gone bad. I briefly mentioned it above and will further explain myself. Think of wine oxidation like a half-eaten apple on your counter at home. What happens to an apple if you take a bite out and set it on your counter? Eventually, it will turn brown. This is because of oxidation. Oxygen encountering the apple and turning it brown or makes it bad. Wine, when left in contact with oxygen also will turn brown or go "bad." Some wines, like some apples take longer than others to oxidize. In fact, in some cultures, oxidation is encouraged in their wine making process (Vin Jaune).

When smelling an oxidized wine, there may be a hint of cider smell to it. When looking at an oxidized wine, it may even appear brown like an apple.

This brings me to smelling and tasting wine at a restaurant. This next section is important!!

When the waiter brings you a bottle, he or she is showing you the bottle for you to acknowledge that is the bottle you ordered. They will then uncork the bottle and present you with the cork. DO NOT smell the cork or worse, lick the cork. The cork will come with identifying marks to ensure the cork in the bottle correlates with the name on the label. This is done because of counterfeiting and not because the cork will tell you anything about the wine. The cork presentation is merely to prove the wine in the bottle is the wine on the label and that you ordered this wine. You will then be poured a small splash of wine. You will look (as instructed above) and swirl and inspect. Now technically, you truly just need to look and smell the wine. This splash is done to ensure you were not given a faulty wine. If you look and smell your wine and it seems "on par" then you can nod in approval and the waiter will begin pouring ladies first.

So, let's repeat that part.

After you order a bottle of wine in a restaurant you will

- Identify wine on the label is the wine you ordered.

- Identify the name on the cork correlates with the label and that you ordered that wine.

- Look for faulty wine.

- Smell for faulty wine.

- Approve or do not approve the bottle.

How to taste wine

As mentioned above when smelling wine, the first sniff is essentially on the house and just used to prepare the nose for a deeper, more thoughtful whiff. Your tongue should be treated the same way. The first sip is to coat the tongue or prepare it for a more useful swish and taste.

As I will go on further to explain, your tongue can essentially taste only five things. Bitter, sweet, salt, sour and Unami. Other than that, most of the tasting you do is through your posterior pharynx and via you nose. Yes, you essentially taste through your nose.

Now, it should make more sense as to why many people, when tasting wine, will open their mouth or swish as if they are using mouthwash. You may even hear some individuals sucking air into their mouth while holding wine in their mouth. All these methods are permitted and even encouraged when appropriately tasting wine. This allows the flavor profile to be sensed on the tongue while also picking up flavors via your posterior pharynx. It also helps if you followed the recommendations above when smelling the bouquet of the wine.

One aspect that your tongue is responsible for is a wine's acidity. Many people love acid and I mean love acid. People who love acid may even mistake their love for acid by saying they prefer "sweet" wines. These individuals who love acid have a special name in the wine community and are typically known as "acid heads." When tasting a wine that is seemingly high in acid, it will make your mouth water. As a grape ripens, it tends to lose some of its acidity. If the grape has a tough time ripening, then it tends to be higher in acidity. That all being said, if the grape is grown in a cooler climate, then it tends to struggle to ripen, and therefore will be more acidic.

If a wine tends to dry your mouth out, that means it is higher in tannins and is a very "tannic" wine. Wines get their tannins from the skin, stems, seeds, and oak. Red wines tend to have higher tannins than white wines because they macerate in their skins and possibly their stems whereas white wines do not tend to come into contact with these elements. A high tannic wine will dry your mouth out because tannins tend to remove a protein from your palate.

Wines that are higher in alcohol tend to taste "hotter" than lower alcohol wines. Higher alcohol wines tend to "burn" on the back of your palate as opposed to their lower-alcohol wine counterparts.

When tasting the wine:

- Take an initial sip to coat the tongue.
- Take a bigger sip and suck air in at the same time to allow the flavors to open
- (Practice with water beforehand so as not to choke or aspirate at the party)
- Identify 3 flavors – ideally different than the 3 you were able to smell
- Does it make your mouth water?
- Does it dry your mouth out?
- Is it hot in the back of your palate?

Conclusions

In the above paragraphs I went onto explain how to look, smell and taste wine. Each element is important onto itself. I will go onto explain the steps to help you work through the progression and sooner or later this will become second nature and you will be tasting wine like you do pizza, without any guide.

Wine	Pizza
Is it a red or white wine?	Round or square?
Is it pale or deep in color?	Thin or deep dish?
What does the rim color look like?	Corn starch on bottom?
Is it a younger or older wine?	Melted cheese or cold cheese?
Are the legs thick or thin?	Thin on sauce or cheese?
Swirl the glass	Too much sauce or cheese?
Quick sniff – coat those nostrils	Burnt edges?
Longer sniff – any fault?	Thick or thin crust?
Identify 3 things you smell	Too hot or cold?
Swirl again	Cheese all fall off the slice?
Take sip – coat the tongue	Cooked or undercooked?
Longer sip – suck air in and swish	Nice crunch or chewy?
Identify 3 things you taste	Clean to eat or make a mess?
Is the wine hot?	
Does it make your mouth water or dry it out?	

Four
Migraines and Wine

Much of my career has revolved around the diagnosis and treatment of migraines. For over a decade I have cared for those individuals that suffer with various types of headaches and I have prescribed several pharmaceutical treatments to either prevent a person from developing a migraine and abort an acute attack of a migraine. Regardless of a patient's migraine frequency or severity, I am typically educating them on the benefits of keeping a migraine diary in order to help identify his or her "triggers." These triggers could be something as simple as stress, dehydration, or even a lack of sleep. But without a doubt, one migraineur, per day, blames red wine for an etiology of a migraine.

To add insult to injury, every patient "knows" what it is about red wine that triggers their headaches. They are all convinced their migraine stems from the sulfites found in the bottle!

"I cannot drink red wine. I just cannot handle the sulfites found in red wine."

What makes them so certain that it is the sulfites? Maybe it is because the label says, "contains sulfites?" Yet, the other ingredients are rarely ever listed.

What if the label said, "contains egg whites?"

What if the label said, "dyed with Mega Purple?"

Would they still blame sulfites if any of the above were listed?

Now it is true that most wines contain sulfites; but it is found in both red and white wine! So, why does red wine take the beating?

It is true some wines contain egg whites to help clear any sediment and yes, it is true many wines we are buying contain Mega Purple.

So, what is it then? What is the cause for the headaches?

Though we are not completely certain, my recommendation is that we should not be so quick to judge that it is the sulfites.

Why are they convinced red wine causes their headaches? Is red wine causing their headache or is this just a misconception? Very similar to the story of Paul Revere. Most people reading this book believe Paul Revere was the gentleman that warned us about the British coming. But I feel it would behoove you to learn about Israel Bissell? Sometimes we just believe what history has told us for years.

"When the legend becomes fact, print the legend." As James Stewart said in *The Man Who Shot Liberty Valance.*

So, the legend is that sulfites cause migraines, so let's just print the legend and blame sulfites.

Is it the sulfites?

Sulfites are typically utilized in the process of wine making to preserve the wine. This is essentially why it is found in most wines; red AND white. Now many wineries (most of which are in France) do not utilize sulfites to stabilize their wine but rather allow nature and time to preserve their wine.

But let us assume the sulfites we are drinking in wine are triggering more migraines. Why are other foods high in sulfites not also as widely blamed? Why are canned fruits and vegetables not blamed in my examination room as the etiology of his or her headaches? Why are my patients not saying, "that damn creamed corn the other night?"

There is an abundance of sulfites in much of what we eat daily, but my patients never blame those foods for causing their migraines. Red wine seems to take the brunt of it; interestingly, since many of these canned goods contain 10 times the number of sulfites compared to wine.

In my opinion, there is nothing to see here. Sulfites are most likely not the cause for most migraines. But if they are, let us also talk about all the canned goods you are also consuming.

Is it histamines?

Histamines play a pivotal role in our body's immune response. Histamine release mediates allergies and a person's allergic response. In other words, histamine release is what we experience when we get that runny nose, facial flushing, or itchy sensation. Histamines are also why some people turn beat red while drinking any wine or alcohol. Red wine typically has a much higher concentration of histamines compared to white wine. However, histamines are also found in fermented foods, such as fish and aged cheeses.

In fact, champagne acts more like white wine in its histamine content as opposed to red wine. Typically, the people of France, by far and away blame Champagne as the cause of their migraines as opposed to red wine like the Americans. So, once again, I doubt it is the histamine release of red wine that is involved with my patient's complaint of increased migraines. Additionally, studies have confirmed the lack of evidence regarding histamine's causation of migraines.

Is it Mega Purple?

So, what is Mega Purple other than a robot sounding name from the future? Mega Purple is a grape concentrate that serves many purposes. It is designed to mask certain vegetal flavors of a wine to make it more palatable for people seeking that "fruit bomb" they expect when we crack open a new red wine. Mega Purple also serves to color-up the wine to achieve the specific pantone (color) our rods and cones expect Cabernet or Syrah to look like.

According to some journal reports, Mega Purple is widely used in many red wines to ensure a more uniform product. For example, Wine X of 2014 will be just like Wine X of 2020 because we created it that way. You want a deep ruby wine? We will give you a deep ruby looking wine. You want a bottle of red fruit? We will make you a bottle of wine that tastes like red fruit. If you want it, we can make it. In a lab that is.

Is it just the alcohol itself?

Some individuals may say that "I avoid alcohol because alcohol, itself gives me a migraine." And you know what? There is some truth to that. One third of migraine patients report alcohol itself as their trigger. In fact, many studies demonstrate migraineurs avoid alcohol more often than control groups. However, low to moderate alcohol consumption has been shown to have health benefits for patients such as migraineurs. Please see Chapter Seven.

The country in which you reside also plays a key role in what you blame for your migraines. If you live in the United Kingdom or United States, you tend to blame red wine but if you live in France or Italy, you will find yourself blaming white wine or Champagne.

One study found that a large amount of red wine (300mL) and not vodka of the equivalent alcohol content provoked a headache. Ah ha!! So, it is red wine then? It is obviously not alcohol, if vodka did not provoke this response. But I would urge caution with that statement because as a medical provider, I can assure you we know very little about how this study was blinded in the first place. For all we know they could have been coaching the witness and those results are in fact not accurate. I mean, who does not know the difference between wine and vodka once it hits your lips?

So, what do we know for certain?

1. Millions of people in this world suffer with migraines.
2. Many migraineurs avoid alcohol because they are convinced it is a trigger for their migraines.
3. If you live in the United States or United Kingdom, you are convinced (without proof) that red wine triggers migraines.
4. f you live in France or Italy, you are convinced (without proof) that white wine or champagne triggers migraines.

So, I ask…

How does red wine in the United States differ from red wine in France or Italy?

Is it alcohol content? No

Is it sulfites? Most likely not

Is it Mega Purple? Possibly

So maybe it is not red wine in general that makes Americans think it causes migraines but rather the artificially dyed red wine we tend to drink.

Five
Wine Shopping

So, you want to go to a wine store or your grocery store without feeling overwhelmed? The goal with this chapter is to try and make your wine shopping experience a little less stressful. (If that is even possible)

Whether you are going to a store specifically designated for beer and wine or just your local grocery store, getting the perfect bottle can be a daunting task. Everyone seems to have roughly the same internal monologue.

What section do I go to?

France?

Cabernet?

But I wanted a Cabernet from France, where is that section?

What does this label even say? Chateau what?

What grape is this wine?

Oh goodness, everyone is looking at me. Forget it, I will just take this one.

After all the talking to yourself and all the preparation and mental anguish you put yourself through, you end up running out of the store with your brand-new bottle of room temperature, non-alcoholic, sparkling grape juice. Oops.

Contrarily, no one seems to get anxious or nervous when looking at the soda isle or the yogurt section of their grocery store, but we all seem to clam up when staring at the labels on a shelf of Sauvignon Blanc. And, let me tell you, with all the yogurt options, I feel overwhelmed.

Why is that and how can we help with that?

First off, I prepared a questionnaire to use that is specifically designed to prepare a person for the task at hand. It has specific questions one should ask themselves before even entering the store. This could be completed before leaving your home or office for the store, but feel free to screenshot this or take a pic and you can prepare in the parking lot prior to entry. I recommend that you review this list before you enter the store because your mind will begin racing the moment you enter. Now, as you practice this questionnaire and the more times you use it, the less you will need it. Trust me

Question 1.   Red or White

What is the occasion or meal?

....

Question 2. What grape variety were you hoping to get?

It is ok if you don't know.

Do you want a dry wine? Really sweet? Or something in between?

....

Question 3. Any specific region (country) you had in mind?

United States? France? Or some other country (many countries make great wines. Countries you may have never thought made wine)

Does the country not matter? Branch out, trust me, it is worth it.

There are great values out there in other countries.

....

Question 4. How much would you like to pay?

This is probably the biggest question because even Cabernet Sauvignon can range from $3 to thousands of dollars. So be honest with yourself and the store. They understand and can help. "I would like to pay $40 for a decent Cab. What do you have?"

....

The next time you go to buy wine, review these questions and your entry into the wine shop/grocery store should be less overwhelming?

How? You may be asking.

Well, try this; enter the store and when you are greeted by someone, you may say.

"Hi, how are you? I am looking for a nice red wine – maybe a Malbec from France and my budget is around $20."

Honestly, for $20 in Cahors, France you can find some amazing wines. I promise you should try them. Some of my favorite. Malbecs from the states are typically around $20 and most cannot hold a candle to those from Cahors. (My opinion of course)

The response you may receive is "oh, I am sorry, we do not have anything from that region in France, but would you want to try an Argentinian Malbec?" Their ratings tend to rival those in France, and I have a few bottles from here.

Even if the store cannot provide with what you asked, they will have alternative recommendations and can quickly steer you towards somewhere close for somewhat the same price point. It truly is remarkable what some preparation can do for you.

By just greeting them, they now know the wine you want and what you are looking to pay.

But what if there is no employee? Let's say you entered a grocery store where the employees are not even old enough to consume alcohol let alone make recommendations for your dinner party.

Sometimes, and just sometimes, the signs the stores put up can be helpful. The signs that say "Cabernet" or "Pinot Noir."

Like I said, doing research beforehand is extremely useful. If you know you want a certain grape then you just find that grape on the signage, but if it is a region that you are after, some grocery stores are even labelled by country or region. One sign may say "California" while another sign may be labelled "Spain."

If you truly want a bottle from France, this can be a tad trickier. In France, most times they will not list the grape on the bottle. Sure, in some regions, like Alsace they do, but that is one of the exceptions.

In France, there are strict wine laws, and those wine laws specify what is allowed and what is not allowed in the bottle.

What do I mean?

Wine laws dictate what the growers grow and what the bottle is permitted to have within it. Therefore, if the region is listed on the bottle, they presume you will know what grape is essentially in that bottle. Unfortunately, many novice wine-drinkers and even some wine experts struggle with this style of labelling. Many American "experts" stay away from French wine and tout "new world" simply because they cannot comprehend French Wine law. And I promise, they are missing out on some exceptional wine. Exceptional wine that costs a fraction of some mediocre "new world" wine.

Bias aside, let's say the bottle says Beaujolais. That is "just" the region in France; it is not a grape. Most likely, nowhere on that label (front or back) will it say what grape is involved in the process of making that special bottle of wine. It is the assumption that we, as the consumers, know the grape found in the region of Beaujolais is almost always Gamay. (Like 90% of the time)

Another example would be in Bordeaux. The label may say Chateau Mouton Rothschild – Pauillac. No place on that label will any varietal be listed. Pauillac is a smaller region in the bigger region of Bordeaux. Even if you get that far, you still need to understand more laws about the region of Bordeaux and even the smaller region of Pauillac.

In the region of Bordeaux, depending on where your vineyard lies in relation to the Gironde estuary, you will be REQUIRED to grow one grape versus another. If your vineyard is located on the right bank (east) of the Gironde estuary, then your red wine will most likely be dominant Merlot or Cabernet Franc. If your vineyard is located on the left bank (west) then your red wine is most likely dominant in Cabernet Sauvignon. The small region of Pauillac is specifically located in the bigger region of Medoc on Bordeaux's left bank, therefore making it, by law, dominant in Cabernet Sauvignon.

Easy right?

Overwhelmed?

I mention this as a joke because I do not expect you to know or remember all of this, but if you wanted an outstanding Bordeaux to go with your party, it would help if you did. However, I do mention it as a reason to ask for help – not many people understand the regionality of wine in France, so it is ok to ask. The employers love helping.

Labels from France can be tricky and if that is not your idea of fun, and you do not have help from a store employee, you may be better off either doing research online beforehand or staying out of that region completely. But I promise you, there is not one person working in that wine store that is not itching to impart some of their knowledge to help you throw an amazing party. Therefore, ask! It is ok, these employees love to nerd-out on wine knowledge. They will not belittle you. In fact, you will learn a lot from them. Sooner or later, you may even recall facts they taught you and impress your dinner party friends about the bottle you picked up. A few parties later, YOU are the wine expert amongst them.

Crazy right?

Not so much, I promise. Again, you must trust me

Wine facts and a little knowledge can go a long way when it comes to party conversation and chit chat. Rarely will someone ever not like a glass of free wine at a party. Well, unless it is a wine tasting party then suddenly everyone becomes a Sommelier and is critical about the ever so miniscule detail.

Most people will praise the wine for one thing or another. Most of the time it is to be nice to their host; especially when they think you took time and energy to select the perfect wine for the occasion. Now if you have a few facts to go with the bottle regarding the region, the grape or even the winemaker, that bottle will go from being "good" to being "exceptional."

What do I mean?

Well, tasting wine is a lot about the experience. The knowledge about the region and its little nuances. Does this region get a lot of rain which tends to make the grape soggy essentially watering down the flavor of the wine? Does this region have vines near a mint field which gives it a slight eucalyptus flavor which can be quite exceptional? (Stag's Leap) Or, maybe you have a little knowledge about the winemaker and his/her tendencies to over oak wine or use no oak when making a wine.

Whatever the nugget you obtain and pass on, it will take the wine from tasting "good" to a full-blown conversation about how exceptional it is. The conversation may even turn into questions about where you got your wine knowledge. Sooner or later, you are recommending bottles that someone recommended to you and that chain reaction just keeps happening.

The adventure into a wine store should never be an anxiety driven experience but viewed as an educational experience.

Novice to Expert

The more you ask, the more you learn.

The more you learn, the more you can teach.

The more you teach, the more you know.

Six
Old World vs New World

I recently had friends over at my house and was touring my, work-in-progress, wine cellar. A few years ago, we finished an area of our basement we specifically ear-marked to be a wine cellar and have slowly been adding to the room. After getting quotes to build wine shelving from local builders, we decided to go with an online company that specifically work with architects to find the perfect wine racks for space provided. In 2021, we finished the first wall and in early 2022, I completed the adjacent wall. As we were completing that second wall, my friend asked how I planned on organizing the two walls of my wine cellar once completed.

Now, with the Type A/OCD personality that I possess, I thought about this very question numerous times during the room's construction. My plan was to have one wall specifically designated for Old World Wines and the adjacent wall for New World Wines. What seemed like an easy answer for me, got a lot more complicated when he asked, well what is the difference? The answer to his simple question became a lot more complicated than just saying United States on one side and France on the other side. This question ended up requiring an hour to discuss the little nuances found in New World Wines and Old-World Wines. So, let's get into some bullet points.

Old World Wine

- Locations
  - ◊ European Countries (France, Spain, Italy, Germany) as well as Middle Eastern countries and Northern Africa
- Flavor Profile
  - ◊ Less fruity and more minerality
  - ◊ Earthy flavor profiles
- Acid
  - ◊ Higher Acid - brighter
- Alcohol
  - ◊ Lower alcohol because of the cooler climates (look at the latitude for the United States and compare it to that of France) Bordeaux, France and Green Bay, Wisconsin are both 44 degrees north – Green Bay is known as the "frozen tundra"
  - ◊ With climate change, however we are seeing higher alcohol wines from Old World countries

New World Wine

- Locations
  - ◊ United States, South American countries, Australia, and South Africa
- Flavor Profile
  - ◊ Fruity flavors and less earthy flavors
  - ◊ More oak flavors because New World tends to use new oak whereas Old World wines tend to use more neutral oak.
  - ◊ Riper flavors – again due to climate
- Acid
  - ◊ Lower acidity because of the alcohol content
- Alcohol
  - ◊ Higher alcohol because of warmer climate
  - ◊ Increase in temp = increase in ripeness

So yes, though my wine cellar will be organized by country, the flavor profiles will also very distinctive on each wall.

However, its organization will be unmatched because, the next time a friend comes over and says, "I am in the mood for a high acid white wine but not too much alcohol" I can easily send him downstairs and say, "Go grab something from the Old-World wall and look for a label that says "Sancerre."

Should be easy to find, right?

Seven
The French Paradox

It has been globally accepted for many years that moderate wine consumption is good for a person's health. Decades ago, my friend's father would refer to his daily glass of wine as his "medicine." I never understood what he meant until I studied medicine and studied wine.

In the early 1990s, researchers began looking into the health benefits of wine and became fascinated by the fact, though the French had higher fat consumption, they had lower incidence of cardiovascular disease. Despite having one of the highest cholesterol diets (breads, cheeses, and sauces), the French had one of the longest life expectancies in the world. Why is that? Before we get into that specific reason, this anomaly became widely known as the "French Paradox."

Discovering what variable was beneficial in the "French Paradox" also took years of research. The focus of these studies eventually steered towards a person's wine consumption. At the time of this study, the French were found to be consuming more wine than Americans. This statistic however no longer holds true. In fact, French wine consumption has dropped nearly 20% over the last 20 years whereas American wine consumption increased more than 50%.

Many variables were investigated at this time. One variable was a person's quantity of wine consumption. Researchers wanted to know if healthier individuals imbibed minimally, moderately, or heavily. They also investigated whether healthier individuals consumed more white, red, or sparkling wine.

The investigators discovered that people who consumed red wine had a lower incidence of coronary artery disease than those who primarily consumed white or sparkling wine. So, what is it about the winemaking process for red wine that differs from white wine?

Well, when making red wine, the juice tends to macerate with the stems, seeds, and skins of the grape. Whereas, when making white wine, the juice comes into little to no contact with the seeds, stems, or skins. Researchers then asked, "what does the skin, seeds or stems contain that would make it healthier?" That answer was easy; RESVEROTROL. Now, commonly referenced as, Grape Seed Extract.

Resveratrol is technically a chemical that is produced by many plants when they react to a threat or an attack. Akin to "You scared the resveratrol out of me!" Get it? Resveratrol is typically seen in the seeds of grapes, peanuts, and blueberries.

The process of making white wine involves carefully separating the juice from the seeds/skin of the grape to preserve the "clear" juice color and produce the "white" wine we all know and love. However, in the making of red wine, the grape is crushed with the seed and skin which most likely releases the chemical called resveratrol. Again, creating the grape to say, "you scared the resveratrol out of me" and releasing that chemical into the juice.

Given the discovery regarding the benefits of resveratrol, many companies attempted to recreate this benefit without the need to consume alcohol. Companies began selling supplements either labeled 'Grape Seed Extract' or 'Resveratrol.' The issue, however, is people were not seeing the same benefit as those consuming red wine. Researchers then needed to investigate what the difference between the resveratrol supplements and red wine and why the wine was beneficial for a person's health, but the supplements were not.

Researchers uncovered that resveratrol is mostly absorbed under the tongue or sublingually therefore making the pills essentially not effective considering it bypasses these sublingual glands. Once the resveratrol hit the stomach, its acids seemed to burn through it essentially minimizing the benefit a person may be expecting to receive. One study even claimed that sublingual absorption was fifteen times more beneficial than the stomach's absorption of resveratrol.

Studies also went on to investigate how much wine do we need to drink in order to receive any of the "French Paradox" benefits. Researchers wanted to know if the amount of red wine needed to receive these health benefits. Researchers found that a moderate consumption of red wine was needed to receive the health benefits advertised above. A "moderate" amount is considered two, 5 ounces glasses of wine for men and one, 5-ounce glass for women.

So, if the benefits of resveratrol are found best absorbed sublingually, then why do we need to drink red wine at all? Why do we not just swish the red wine and then spit it out?

I would say that we absolutely could infer this to be true.

Though considered oversimplifying the data, I would absolutely infer that is exactly what the researchers uncovered.

To summarize,

- Red wine was more beneficial than white or sparkling wine
- Resveratrol is the chemical found to be responsible for the health benefits
- 15 times more resveratrol is absorbed under the tongue than in the stomach.
- A moderate amount of red wine is most beneficial (one - two, 5 oz glasses).

Therefore, theoretically, a person could take 1-2 glasses of red wine, swish it around for a few seconds and spit it out and receive much more of a health benefit than a person who takes resveratrol supplements and/or swallows 1-2 glasses of red wine.

Before I started my classes to complete my first wine certification, I reached out to the school and asked,

"If I am going to be tasting 10 wines every week, how am I supposed to be driving home?"

A reasonable question I thought, but the laughter could have been heard miles away.

"Oh Jesse, we do not drink the wine in class. Each splash is one ounce, and we typically swish and spit it out in class."

At the time, I thought that to be a tremendous waste of good wine, but as the classwork began, I understood how I would not be able to stand had I consumed all that wine let alone drive 60+ minutes home. Knowing what I know now, the health benefit we must have received is immeasurable! Each splash for tasting was about 1 ounce and if you take the 10 wine we tasted, that would be ten, 1-ounce pours therefore being the equivalent to "two, 5-ounce glasses of wine!"

Just the right amount!

Outstanding!

Eight
Temperature To Serve Wine

There has always been a debate as to what temperature is the best temperature to serve wine. Whether it be red or white, the temperature can be the difference between an exceptional wine and a "so so" bottle. For example, if you happen to leave a bottle in your car while it is 90 degrees out, what do you expect to happen to it? That's right, it will spoil. Now, if you take that same wine and chill it down, what will happen? Most likely, the cooler temps will diminish any flavor that wine originally possessed. Instead, you will taste just a cool, possibly refreshing, alcoholic-filled juice.

Temperature matters in multiple facets of wine consumption. Aside from the obvious, wine tasting, temperature matters when it comes to shipping and transportation as well as storage. Certainly, I would not recommend shipping wine when it is 20 below zero Fahrenheit just as I would not advise shipping a case when it is north of 75 degrees Fahrenheit.

In matters of storage, your dining room and bedroom closet are not ideal places for wine to be stored, but rather consider a temperature regulated basement. If a temperature-controlled basement is not an option then buying bottles as you drink is sometimes a person's best option.

In this chapter, I will lay out bullet points regarding the recommendation for serving red wine, white wine as well as sparkling wine. Within each category there are smaller subset and more specified recommendations.

As stated in other chapters, this is to serve as a guide and not an absolute. These are my recommendations and my preference, but you may find a range of temperature that you prefer.

Red Wine

Usually, recommended to be served at "room" temperature.

Now this was room temperature when the 'room' was a cellar which is notably cooler than most homes.

Rule of thumb – 50 degrees Fahrenheit to 65 degrees Fahrenheit.

The less bold the wine, the cooler it should be.

The bolder the wine, the warmer it should be served.

Pinot Noir – ideally served closer to 50 degrees Fahrenheit

Cabernet Sauvignon – ideally served closer to 65 degrees Fahrenheit

White Wine

Rule of thumb – 45 degrees Fahrenheit to 55 degrees Fahrenheit

The 'zippier' the white wine, the cooler it should be

Your fresh, eye-popping Sauvignon Blanc should be closer to 45 degrees Fahrenheit

The more oaky the white wine, the closer to 55 degrees Fahrenheit you want it

Your oaked Chardonnay may be 55 degrees Fahrenheit as an example. But your stainless steel Chardonnay, closer to 45 degrees Fahrenheit.

Sparkling Wine

Typically, this should be served between 35 degrees Fahrenheit and 45 degrees Fahrenheit. Nice, cool, and refreshing.

Like the above white wine recommendations, the more oaked/age worthy Champagnes should be served closer to 45 degrees Fahrenheit, but your more wallet-friendly Proseccos should be served closer to 35 degrees Fahrenheit.

The Wine Doctor

Nine
Bottle Sizes

187.5 mL   Split bottle

     Equivalent to one glass of wine

375 mL   Half bottle or Demi

     Equivalent to two glasses of wine

750 mL   **The standard bottle size for most wine**

     Equivalent to 4-6 glasses of wine

1.5 L   Magnum

     Equivalent to two standard bottles

     Equivalent to 8-12 glasses of wine

3.0 L   Double magnum or Jeroboam in Champagne

     Equivalent to 4 standard bottles

     Jeroboam translates to "First King of this Kingdom"

4.5 L   Rehoboam in Champagne

         Equivalent to 6 standard bottles

6 L   Methuselah

         Equivalent to 8 standard bottles

         Methuselah translates to "The Oldest Man"

9 L   Salmanzar

         Equivalent to 12 standard bottles

         Salmanzar translates to the "King of Assyria"

12 L   Balthazar

         Equivalent to 16 standard bottles

         Balthazar translates to the "One of the Wise Men"

15 L   Nebuchanezzar

         20 standard bottles

         Nebuchanezzar translates to the "King of Babylon"

20 L   Solomon

         Equivalent to 26 standard bottles

         Solomon translates to the "King of Solomon"

30 L   Melchizedek

         Equivalent to 40 standard bottles

         Melchizedek translates to "The Truthful King"

*Berringer created the "Maximus" size for charity in 2001. It was 130 L which is equivalent to 184 standard bottles or 15 cases of wine. (One bottle was equal to 15 cases of wine).

Yes, ONE bottle was equivalent to 15 CASES of wine (180 bottles of wine).

Ten
The Sideways Effect – The Joke Everyone Missed

Many wine connoisseurs have at the very least a small understanding of what is called the "Sideways Effect." The "Sideways Effect" happened in 2004 with the Fox Searchlight Pictures' release of the movie Sideways. In this dramatic comedy starring Paul Giamatti and Thomas Hayden Church, two friends travel to wine country for a few days away as bachelors before one of them (Thomas Hayden Church) is set to be married. The movie reached critical acclaim and was up for several Academy Awards. These nominations included

Best Picture

Best Director

Best Supporting Actor

Best Supporting Actress

And it did win the Oscar for Best Adapted Screenplay.

There were many memorable moments in the movie, but what most wine lovers recall is that this movie single handedly boosted Pinot Noir consumption and production in the United States while also tarnishing one of the world's best grapes in the process. The grape that suffered.? Merlot. This boost of Pinot Noir consumption and the collapse of Merlot consumption is in fact, the "Sideways Effect."

Now, you may be asking, how did a fictional movie have that kind of impact on the wine industry?

Well, for those that do not know, the movie focused a lot on Paul Giamatti's character (Miles) and his passion for Pinot Noir. He describes in detail, his respect for the grape and how difficult it is to produce while also destroying the reputation of Merlot. At one point, he goes as far to say, "I am not drinking any ****ing Merlot." I left the expletive out for the children. If you appreciate the grape Pinot Noir for being fragile and finicky then you also appreciate the fact that Paul's character is too very fragile and finicky. Paul, in fact, is Pinot Noir.

The most ironic part about his disdain for Merlot and why I feel his entire rant was meant to be a joke was because of what occurred during a brief scene most people, including wine connoisseurs, missed. Now even the most sophisticated wine lover may have also missed the joke if their knowledge of French wine is not up to snuff. To understand the joke, a person would need knowledge regarding Bordeaux and its left and right banks of the Gironde Estuary.

What was the joke you ask?

Well, Virginia Madsen (Maya) and Paul Giamatti (Miles) returned to her friend's house after dinner and are discussing the most prized wines in their collection as well as bottles that changed their view on wine. This bottle is also known to wine lovers as the bottle that hooked them or the bottle that changed their life.

Sandra Oh yells out to them from the other room that they can open anything but her Richebourg. Richebourg is a Grand Cru from the region of Cote de Nuit in Bourgogne France. That's right, you guessed it, a Pinot Noir.

Maya discusses the bottle that changed her view on wine which was the 1988 Sassicaia. The Sassicaia is a Super Tuscan which is akin to a Bordeaux Blend – and this specific bottle tends to have a blend of Cabernet Sauvignon and Cabernet Franc.

Miles, on the other hand, very unexpectedly states the prize in his collection was a 1961 Cheval Blanc. Maya then asks him why he did not bring it or for him to leave and go get it. He goes on to say that he has not had any special occasion to open it. Maya states that the day you open the bottle of 1961 Cheval Blanc IS the special occasion. And I personally could not agree more as I discuss in Chapter 14.

Now, do not let the name fool you. There is no "Blanc" in Cheval Blanc. It is not a white wine, but rather, Cheval Blanc is a RED wine from the right bank of the Gironde Estuary in Bordeaux. The right bank of the Estuary is typically a blend with the wine being dominant in either Merlot or Cabernet Franc. Cheval Blanc specifically is typically around half Merlot and half Cabernet Franc. (A few small percentages of Cabernet Sauvignon may also be found which will lower either the Cabernet Franc or Merlot in its blend). It all depends on the year.

MERLOT!! You say??? But Miles hates Merlot and refused to drink Merlot. Again, he said "I am not drinking any ****ing Merlot" pretty emphatically before dinner that evening.

Yes, the most prized wine in his possession is a Bordeaux Blend where Merlot is one of the dominant grapes? The moment he mentioned that the 1961 Cheval Blanc as his most prized wine possession literally occurred a few minutes after his rant about refusing to drink any Merlot if the ladies ordered it. Funny? On purpose? Maybe

Unfortunately, almost every one of the viewers (wine connoisseurs included) did not understand that Cheval Blanc is NOT a white wine let alone its blending technique being dominant in Merlot.

With this knowledge, it makes the joke of him hating Merlot that much funnier. But it is not funny when one of the world's greatest wine grapes, Merlot, has its reputation destroyed because of a joke that nobody got.

In the year following the release of Sideways, Pinot Noir production in California rose 170% and is now the second most widely planted varietal in Sonoma County. In that same calendar year, Merlot in California saw its sales drop 21%.

In one aspect, it is hard to believe that a fictional movie about wine could influence production/consumption the way Sideways has, but in another sense, it is not all that unbelievable.

What I do find amazing and almost appalling is that so many "wine experts" tried to justify Miles' belief regarding Pinot Noir vs Merlot. The wine community would develop arguments about the grape's finicky nature as to where it is grown, or the thin skin it has that makes it difficult to produce. All these arguments were used as an attempt to justify how wise Miles was in his belief that Pinot Noir was the most superior varietal that ever existed. Me on the other hand, I am thrilled to get deals on bottles of Merlot. Which, by far and away is one of my favorite varieties.

Eleven
Does the wine glass matter?

When people I work with realize that I have a little bit of wine knowledge they tend to ask me the same two questions.

1. What is your favorite wine – (Chateau d'Yquem for white and Heitz Martha's Vineyard for red)

2. Does the glass really matter?

The short answer to the second question is a simple "yes." But the detailed answer is a lot more complicated than just yes. There is a multitude of reasons why the glass matters, but I will attempt to touch on three overarching reasons.

Aroma

Temperature

Flavor

Aroma

Many poke fun at the people tasting wine by swirling their glass and sticking their nose all the way into the glass, but there is a very specific purpose for this. Using this method to drink wine is not intended to just look pretentious. You truly only taste five sensations using your tongue, bitter, sweet, salt, sour and Unami. All the fancy flavors people describe in detail when "tasting" wine is mostly from a person's nose. This is how we truly smell our food and wine. Therefore, there is great benefit by sticking your "schnoz" in the opening of the glass well before tasting the wine. Sometimes, a person may even smell a wine multiple times before ever even taking their first sip.

A person could then argue that all glasses should be wide and deep; to get the nose inside, right? Well, not exactly, for reasons to be explained under temperature but also in this section. Bolder flavors tend to be more complex and need more time and more space to develop. Red wines tend to have bolder aromas and therefore benefit from a wide rimmed large opening glassware.

White wines tend to have more flowery aromas and benefit from smaller opening glasses. They also tend to be served cooler making the aroma a little tighter as compared to a red wine. Smaller, more narrow wine glasses tend to bring the wine closer to the nose and therefore easier to pick up certain aromas. Especially when the wine is cooler, and its aromas are much tighter.

Temperature

Because red wine is typically served at warmer temperatures compared to white wines, it makes more sense for red wine to be in a wider, deeper bowl glass. Red wine is typically served at room temperature therefore can be in a larger style glass.

White wines tend to be served cooler and benefit by a smaller glass because it aids in preserving the wine's cooler temperature.

Stemless glasses are fancy looking and seem to be easier to grip. However, the palm of your hand tends to heat up the glass. If the glass gets warmer, so does your wine. Therefore, stemless wine glasses tend to heat up wines sooner than originally intended. This may diminish the wines flavor and allow it to spoil much sooner than originally intended.

With spoilage, think of an apple and a half-eaten apple that are sitting on your counter. The fully intact apple can sit there for hours if not days and still be good. The half-eaten apple, however, may last an hour or two before turning brown (oxidizing) and no longer being plateable. Now, I am not saying you have days to drink wine sitting in a stemmed glass versus a stemless glass, but you get my point.

Flavor

A deeper, wider glass tends to allow more wine to be in contact with the air or oxygen. By allowing this, a person is allowing the wine to soften and making it more palatable. With high tannic wines, allowing more contact with air makes it drinkable sooner. In addition, bolder red wines benefit by heavy swirling and require a wider opening to do so.

More contact with the air allows more wine to "breath." When a wine breathes it opens-up. And, when a wine opens-up, it is easier to drink and identify the layers of flavor within.

White wines tend to benefit from smaller glasses to preserve its cooler temperature and therefore making it crispier or tarter. By allowing less air contact, white wines tend to open-up less which is beneficial given its low-tannic profile.

The rim of the glass also matters when it comes to tasting wine for a few different reasons. Many glasses, if you run your fingers along the rim, will have a rounded like structure at the tip. One reason this lip may be present is the mechanical device used to manufacture the glass. The cheaper the equipment used to manufacture the glass, the larger the rounded tip tends to be.

Also, pay attention to which side of the glass the rounded tip is located. Is it on the inside of the opening of the glass or is it on the outside? Why is this important? Well, it is as simple as the fact it creates an obstacle for your wine as it enters your palate. A speed bump if you will. As you swirl your wine (and attempt to keep it in the glass) you will also eventually lift that glass to your mouth. The more obstacles in its way, the more impedance to its true flavor you experience. Therefore, if the rounded tip is on the inside of the opening, that can be problematic. Some of your best glasses have no rounding whatsoever. When shopping for wine glasses, keep this in mind.

The perfect glass

To maximize your experience when drinking wine, a person is most likely going to want ….

A stemmed glass - so the temperature of wine is not altered by the heat of your hand.

A glass with little to no lip on the rim or if you must have a lip, one located on the outside of the bowl as opposed to the inside.

For red wine - a bigger bowled glass to open it up more which will enhance the tasting experience from how it smells to what flavors you appreciate.

For white wine - a smaller bowled glass to preserve temperature and bring the more floral/citrus notes in the wine close to your nose to enhance your wine drinking experience.

Twelve
Serving Wine

Though serving wine can be a daunting task, my hope with the following is to make it easy and understandable. Though there is some beauty to the methods of opening a bottle of wine, sometimes all you want is to get at that good stuff. There are a variety of methods and bottle openers to use. Typically, and most commonly, individuals will have a version of a waiter's key. A waiter's key usually has a duller knife at one end while also have the corkscrew at the other. The dull knife is for cutting the foil wrapper off the bottle or digging at the wax enclosure. The screw end of the key is, you guessed it, for opening the wine. Hence the word "key."

With the knife part of the "waiter's key" start by cutting the foil above or below the lip of the bottle. Typically, it is cut below the lip by either is acceptable. For a more professional opening, cut below the lip. In my opinion, it looks cleaner.

Insert the screw part of the key into the center of the cork turning it multiple times (about 75% of the way into the cork) while then gently pulling the cork straight out. The idea is to NOT screw the key past the other side of the cork. This will send cork fragments into the wine, and no one wants that. Also, be careful to not break/crack the cork when pulling it out. This will take practice and some bottles require a lot of patience. After opening, present the cork to your guest who selected the bottle.

When opening a screw-capped wine, twist the screw cap until open. (Yes, this was meant to be a joke).

However, this brings us to the next argument. Screw cap or cork?

Cork vs Screw Cap

Though there tends to be a stigma regarding screwcaps, the future is most likely heading in that direction. By having a screwcap, vineyards have more control over how their wine tastes therefore, outside of good ole nostalgia, makes screw caps preferred. Screw caps prevent even micro-oxygenation from occurring and therefore taking one variable out of the mix when it comes to the flavor profile of their wine. Unlike corks, screw caps do not crack, break, or shrink. There is little to no risk of damage to the wine when opening a screwcap. You cannot poke through the other side of the cork when opening nor can you break tiny fragments into your expensive bottle of Cabernet.

Corks are beneficial because historically it has "always" been done that way. There is some semblance of nostalgia when it comes to corks. The romance of opening a bottle of wine comes with having a cork as well. Using a cork allows the wine to age because of its micro-oxygenation. This sometimes is the biggest benefit of corking a bottle of wine.

Though wines are viewed as "cheap" because they use a screwcap, these stigmas are changing, and more and more vineyards will start using them. Many vineyards still prefer the micro-oxygenation and prefer the natural resource the cork does provide.

Personally, I prefer the romance of the cork. There is just something special about using a wine-opener (a key), cutting the foil, and uncorking that bottle. It is a skill, and many rely on the wine-expert to properly open their bottle at home as well as in restaurants. Opening a bottle with a cork is also part of the "show" sommelier's use in restaurants while having a conversation about the wine. Many sommeliers provide his/her guest a history about that specific bottle or its vineyard or vigneron while opening the bottle. If a screwcap is the future, then this art may and will be lost.

Decanting

Decanting is a process where you pour your bottle of wine into a larger, typically fancier glass serving piece. Though it makes the wine look fancy, it does serve a specific purpose. When a wine is young, high in tannins and just not ready to drink, by decanting the wine, you will make it more palatable sooner. By exposing the wine to oxygen, you will allow the acids to lessen, the tannins to soften and make the wine more drinkable. Some wines take longer than others. But as a rule of thumb, once decanted, allow for a minimum of 20-30 minutes.

White wine historically does not need too much decanting though it is possible depending on the wine and the winemaking process.

Champagne or other Sparkling Wine

Opening a bottle of sparkling wine is certainly a special occasion. Though it can be dangerous, if certain precautions are taken then the beauty and mystique of opening that bottle will be preserved.

- First, ensure the bottle is chilled. Ideally, it should be around 45-60 degrees Fahrenheit. This can be achieved by purchasing a wine fridge and set the temperature to 45 degrees Fahrenheit. You can also get a champagne bucket, fill it with ice, add salt and water and wait 15 minutes. You can also (though not encouraged) place the bottle in the fridge for a few hours. Most refrigerators are set for 40 degrees Fahrenheit. Though cooler, it will be ok but also takes some planning ahead. Essentially, have a good idea of when you plan to open the bottle and work backwards when calculating a time to set in the refrigerator.

- Once chilled, remove the foil wrapping

- As you begin to unscrew the cage – (typically 6 twists of the cage lock) – ensure your hand is securely holding the cork to prevent it from unexpectedly flying out and hurting someone or breaking something. Do not remove the cage. A cork typically "shoots" out at 65mph and can really hurt someone or something if these precautions are not taken.

- Hold the bottle at a 45-degree angle – gripping the cork in your left hand while holding the bottle in your right hand. (Reverse this language if you are left-handed)

- While holding the cork and the opened cage in your left palm, gently twits THE BOTTLE and not the cork. NOT THE CORK. After a few twists, the cork should gently release from the bottle.

- One wine course I took once said opening a bottle of Champagne should sound like the whisper of a princess as opposed to the fart of a whore and I absolutely loved that. So, let's keep that recommendation. Though, in movies, the louder the "pop" the more fun the party.

Another way to open a bottle of sparkling wine is via a saber, a sword or even a simple wine glass. While holding the champagne bottle at a 45-degree angle, if a person briskly swipes any one of these items along the bottle and clips the lip at the neck of the bottle, the bottle should separate along that seem while in fact opening the bottle. Though this method may take some practice, it is quite "useful" and quite entertaining at parties. It is by no means practical because glass tends to go everywhere and the Champagne may fly out as well, but it looks super cool that is for sure.

Thirteen
Organic Wine Movement

Nowadays with everyone being more environmentally conscious and companies focusing on sustainability, why would we think the wine industry would be any different?

Every day, I am in my office discussing with patients my version of what I call the "risk/benefit ratio." This ratio is how I determine if/when a patient may need medication. The benefit of a pharmaceutical must outweigh the risk or the side effect. A common question I receive when discussing medications with patients is not what can this drug do FOR me; but rather, they ask, what is this drug going to do TO me?

For me to recommend a medication to a patient, his or her benefit of the medication must outweigh any potential risk or side effect. Now, this is not always full proof, there is a risk the medication is not as successful as we hope or the risk the patient may be unknowingly allergic to the substance, but for the most part, the drug's safety profile is stable, and the risk is minimized or at least lower than the drug's possible benefit.

Wine is made with not just grapes and yeast but countless other chemicals. Some chemicals may be in the bottle, some may be used before the juice ever gets to the bottle or before the grape is even plucked from the vine. The world is shifting, and more and more wineries are becoming more conscious of their environment and surroundings. Why? Well, it is essentially self-preservation.

For decades, if not centuries, vineyards were always harvested at a certain date and a certain time. And typically this harvest would follow the lunar cycle.

Ummmmm, that is why it is called the "HARVEST MOON."

However, as temperatures across the world rise, the harvest date needs pushed back to ensure the grape is reaching its full potential. By pushing the harvest date back a few weeks, you also shorten the vines dormancy. As climates shift, frost risk and other dangerous weather patterns occur with increasing frequency. This is essentially lowering the yields (number of grapes obtained from harvest), most vignerons obtain.

By decreasing chemicals, pesticides and shifting to a more organic or biodynamic process, you may limit climate change then, in turn, preserving your business while also preserving one's health.

However, like anything in life, by improving one aspect of the process, you may also be sacrificing another. The old, "cut your nose off to spite your face" idiom.

In this chapter, we will touch on the difference between organic and biodynamic and what to expect moving forward. But, to understand what they are changing, it is vital to first understand the winemaking process.

Winemaking Process

The winemaking process starts in the vineyard long before you even have grapes. Sometimes it can take three to five years of vineyard preparation before an estate can harvest enough grapes to begin making estate specific wine. This is for a multitude of reasons but mainly soil preparation and vine maturity.

Like any farmer who wants to grow a crop of some kind, they must first plough, level and fertilize the land before planting anything. Sometimes they even need to plant one crop one year to better prepare the land for the crop they want the following year.

Once the soil is prepped and the crop is grown, the harvest is the next step. Typically beginning in fall, collecting all the fruit is done a variety of different ways. Some vineyards mechanize the harvest by using machines to collect all the berries. Some vineyards have the resources to hand pick and select the specific grapes they want from the vine. This ensures no "bad" ones enter the batch. This method can be very costly (because of labor) which then tends to increase the cost of the wine in the bottle. Some vines are harvested before other vines based on the Brix (sugar) content. Most vignerons have a tool to measure this.

After harvest is complete, the juice is fermented and at times aged for a period. After aging, the wine is bottled and eventually distributed. Every step along the way has a purpose and can be manipulated as a vigneron or a vineyard need. Again, as vineyards shift to more organic or biodynamic practices, each step in this process needs some changing. The reason that vineyards require change in each step of the winemaking process is because of organic/biodynamic certification. To be certified "organic" or "biodynamic," each step of the process must be in compliance. Most vineyards take years to completely transition because one step in the process was manipulated at a time. By slowly changing one step at a time, this ensures a similar more uniform product from year to year. Over a few years, each step was changed and then vineyards qualify for certification and approval to utilize the "organic" label on their packaging/bottling.

So, what exactly is the difference between a wine being organic and one being biodynamic?

Organic

What makes a wine organic? Well, I guess the first question should be is the wine organic or is it a wine made with organic grapes? Wait, what??

Yes, that is correct there are a variety of different "organics" that mean a variety of different things.

Just like your garden, bugs, animals, and weeds want their fair share of space. Typically, pesticides are used to prevent rot and limit crop loss from animal or bug consumption. Vineyards that go organic typically use other options to prevent weeds and limit access to animals or insects. Instead of harmful chemicals or pesticides, more natural fertilizer is used such as compost. To protect the crop from insects and other wildlife, the vineyard typically plants other crops in between the vines. Sometimes, these plants could be flowers. These "distractions" per se function not too dissimilar to a rodeo clown. In a rodeo, when the rider falls off the bull, a clown will run out and become the distraction so the rider can escape unharmed. In an organic vineyard, crops are typically grown in between the vines so that bugs, insects, and other animals will feast on them while leaving the majority of the grape crop alone.

During the winemaking process, it is quite common for sulfites to be used. Sulfites help preserve the wine. This chemical reaction typically limits oxidation and functions as an antimicrobial (protecting the wine from bacteria). Typically, your canned vegetables also have sulfites to function as a preservative. In fact, your canned vegetables tend have ten times the number of sulfites as your bottle of wine. Please see the chapter regarding migraines.

In France, there are many regions that do not use sulfites as a preservative but rather allow time and lack of movement to be their preservative. Whatever the method, adding chemicals at any point in the process is disallowed in the organic winemaking process.

Now, that all being said, it can be common for a bottle to state "made with organic grapes." Essentially, this means that the grapes and the vineyard are organic, but chemicals may be used as a preservative, which in turn increases the shelf life.

But wine collectors enjoy collecting and storing their wine. They enjoy the aging process and the flavor that comes when a wine as permitted to age. By going completely organic, this hampers that process and those flavors. So, for some, organic is not the ideal option. Because most of these wines do not have a shelf-life for long-term aging.

For a vineyard to be allowed to claim that they are organic, the vineyard must be free of all pesticides for a minimum of three years. All the yeast and other ingredients a vigneron may use in the winemaking process must also be organic and grown organically. During the winemaking process – fermentation, siphoning, aerating, transportation and distribution, the equipment must also be certified organic. This essentially means it does not encounter any other non-organic material. The vats used to make organic wine can only ever be used to make organic wine.

Biodynamic

Now, biodynamic winemaking is not too dissimilar to organic, but it typically follows the lunar cycle, and the focus is not just on the grape itself but all aspects of the land. The trees, the soil, the bottling and even the transportation.

I personally like the lunar cycle aspect of the biodynamic winemaking. My favorite wine story is the origination of the phrase "honeymoon." Many of us know the word "honeymoon" to be associated with a wedding and the vacation a newly married couple takes typically shortly after they say their 'I Dos'. But that is not what the term "honeymoon's" original intent. It was customary for the father of the bride to ferment enough Honey Mead to last the newly married couple from one full moon to the next full moon. Hence the term "Honeymoon."

Where biodynamic winemaking can sometimes veer off track and seem bizarre to most is when it comes to the soil treatment. In this process, it is not just using organic material or planting distraction plants amongst the vines, but rather it is how they "cure" the vineyard. This curing process improves the soil's viability and strength. Some vignerons report adding deceased animal's skulls and bones to the soil to improve carbon and other chemicals the soil may be deficient in.

When it comes to planting and harvesting as well as pruning, the vineyards follow the lunar cycle as a guide to when these phases need to occur in the winemaking process. Again, no artificial chemicals can used along the way and no sulfites are permitted in storage.

Conclusion

In my neurology practice I have always half-jokingly said that the hospital gets crazy when it is a full moon. Though I kid, I promise you that it absolutely is busier than other weeks. I have also personally noted people complain of more migraines and noted to have more seizures amongst these full-moon days. Though there have been countless studies refuting this cause, it is my personal belief that there is something to the earth's lunar pull and its effect on our health. Why would we believe the grapes are any different?

The vines are a living, breathing thing. The oceans rise and fall with the moon's lunar pull. The waves grow and surfers vie for that ultimate break the moon creates. Our grapes and their vines most likely do the same thing. They are starving for more sunlight, more water and maybe the lunar pull. Though for centuries our ancestors never had a watch or the calendar we know of today. Instead, they used the sun and the moon to guide them in the vineyard. Some of the practices in the organic and biodynamic process does not come without historical perspective but some individuals still do not appreciate the product it produces. Well, that seems to be changing. With the world concerned with global warming and many becoming more sustainability conscious, many vineyards too are shifting their practices. Whether it be organic, biodynamic or the more conventional way of making wine that is your fancy, the process continues to evolve and are most likely never going away. If anything, more vineyards are adapting to these styles and soon you will start seeing more and more organic and biodynamic wines in your local stores.

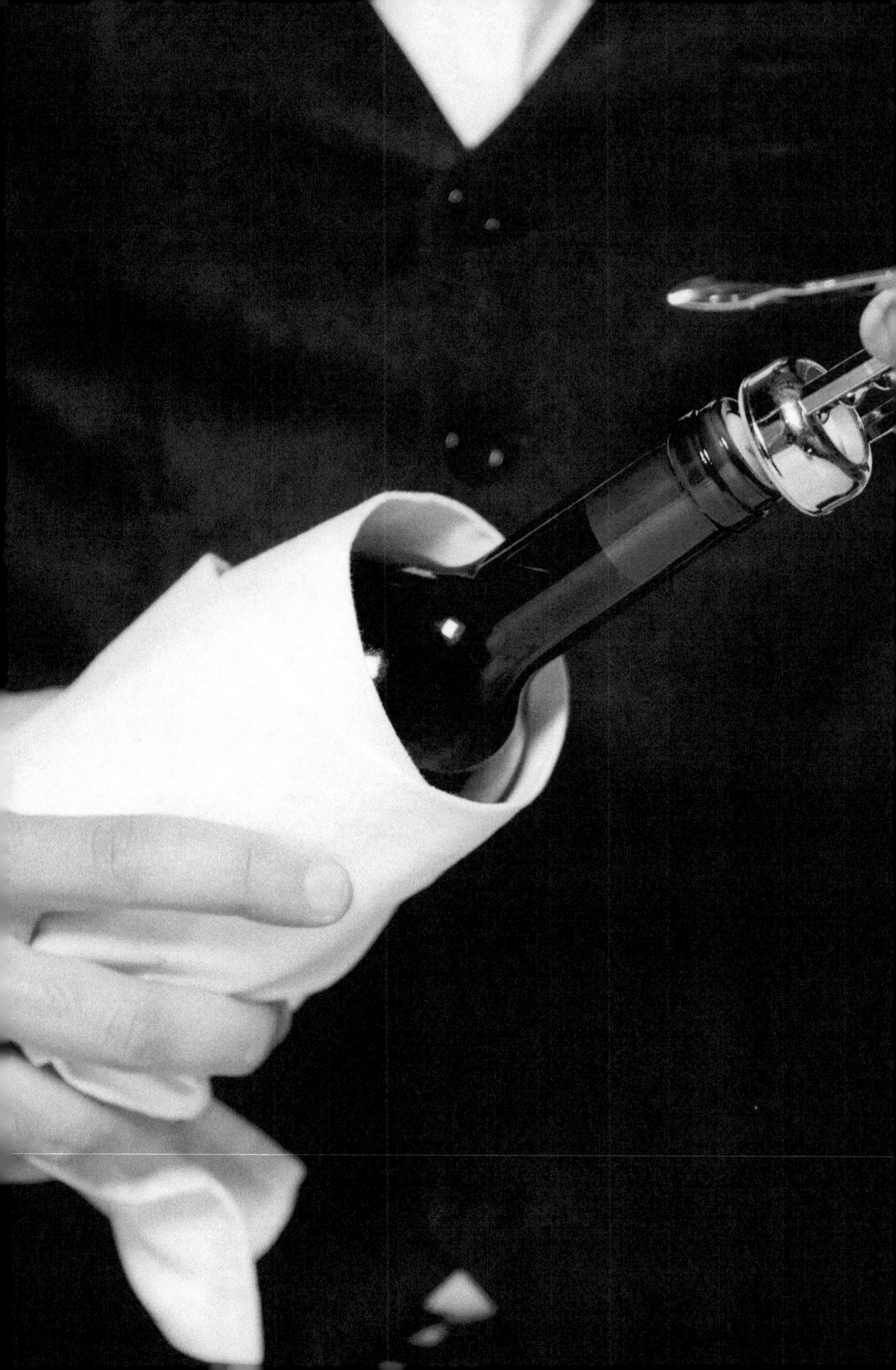

Fourteen
When is the right time to open a bottle of wine?

Whether I am rounding at the hospital or teaching a wine course, a wine question I receive often is, "what wine should I serve with….. chicken/steak/ potato chips?"

Now, if they are asking what wine goes with their potato chips, my answer is always, without hesitation, Champagne. Please do not criticize this combination until you at least try it, once. It will change your life. It truly is spectacular. I promise.

One of the things I use to struggle with was deciding when the right time was to open a great bottle of wine. And by "great" I mean expensive. Do we open this bottle because my uncle, who comes in once a year, is visiting from California? Or do we open the bottle because it is Friday, and I just want to treat myself? Whatever the reason may be, I believe that there are specific moments when it makes sense to crack that special bottle you have been saving for months/years or even decades.

My hope is to help you understand what my specific thought process is – whether you agree with me or not, this is how I tend to utilize my wine cellar and open the wines within it.

In this chapter, I will discuss a few options. (Prices are local to me at the time of writing this book)

1. $200 bottle of Dom Perignon – Tête de Cuvée from Moet & Chandon

2. $70 bottle Moet & Chandon Rose

3. $250 bottle of Heitz Martha's Vineyard

4. $70 bottle of Heitz Cabernet Sauvignon (not Martha's Vineyard/Trailside or Linda Falls)

I live by the mindset that a 'nice' bottle is not just for special occasions, but rather that opening a nice bottle IS the special occasion. Sure, I could have selected a few Bourgogne bottles or Bordeaux bottles from my collection to discuss in this article, but these are not typical bottles found in most wine shops or grocery stores and I wanted to select bottles you can easily find or may already own.

$200 Bottle of Dom Perignon

So, when is the best time to crack open that bottle of "Dom" that you have been saving? Do you open it when you get a promotion or a raise? Do you open it at someone's graduation party? How about at your wedding, is that a good time to open the bottle?

I do not feel any of these events are good occasions to crack the crème de la crème (tête de cuvée) open.

You disagree? Well, hear me out on this one.

When you get a job promotion and/or a raise; what are you going to remember? The new job? The raise? How excited your family was or how excited you were to tell them? I have no clue what the most meaningful aspect of the promotion will be for you, but I can predict what you will most likely not remember; the bouquet of the freshly opened bottle you were storing for the last 5 or 10 years. I can almost guarantee that amongst the excitement of the day, you will not recall the little nuances that differentiate it from your average bottle of Champagne. Why "waste" it on an occasion where it will serve as third or even fourth fiddle? The little intricacies of this bottle will be lost that day. Taking precedent in your memories will be (and rightfully so)

1. Your family's reaction when you told them that you got promoted.

2. The percentage raise in the salary that you received.

3. The respect your employer showed giving you more responsibility

4. Your reaction when they told you that you were getting promoted.

5. ?

6. ?

7. ?

8. We finally opened the Dom

Sure, you may be different and maybe the Dom will be #1 on that list, but I doubt it.

Instead, this would be the great opportunity to crack open your $70 Bottle of Moet & Chandon Rosé. It is pricey enough you feel like you are opening a special bottle but not too pricey where you do not have a second in reserve or the ability to run out and grab a replacement with that new flush raise you just received. Plus, this bottle is incredible, and you will very much enjoy it.

I believe that when you open the Dom, THAT is the special occasion. You may even reflect on the day that you opened the Dom very similarly to the day you received the promotion. I, at least feel the conversation could be similar.

"Remember when I got the promotion? How awesome was it? I worked so hard to achieve this promotion, I am so glad it happened for me."

"Remember when we opened that 2010 Dom? How amazing was it? Remember the extra nutty notes it demonstrated? We worked hard to obtain this bottle and boy was it worth it."

The Dom itself should be the occasion. Have friends and family over if you want but schedule it out – "honey, next Saturday, let's go to dinner, come home, and enjoy the Dom we have been saving. Because why not?"

$250 Bottle of Heitz Martha's Vineyard

Not too indifferent from the recommendation above, I do not advise opening the Martha's Vineyard with any old dinner. Though I am a firm believer that Martha's Vineyard will go well with anything. You truly want the day you open it to be the special occasion.

The question you should be asking is, what should we serve with the Martha's Vineyard, and not will Martha's Vineyard go with this?

What's the difference?

Allow me to explain.

You want to host a dinner party for some friends who enjoy good food and good wine. Do you …select the wine or the meal first? Well, this decision should impact which bottle you recommend.

If you plan on throwing a dinner party because you want to accentuate the local restaurant and their filet medallions, then this could be tricky. If your guests have never had this restaurant's medallions, then maybe this is not a good time to decant the Martha's Vineyard. However, if everyone at the party are regulars to this chef's restaurant and are familiar with his/her cuisine then maybe the purpose of the party is to open the Martha's Vineyard while serving those steak medallions. But, if the guests never had the medallions, then maybe you want to feature the cuisine and could use the entry level Heitz bottle at $70. This would then save the Martha's for another dinner party where it can be front and center.

Again, you want to remember nuances in the wine as opposed to "just" the occasion in which you served the wine.

Recently, my wife and I hosted a dinner party with friends who also enjoy and appreciate good wine. We all have our specific preferences and beliefs, and the goal was to put them aside, taste some great wine and finally end the argument as to who and where did it better. Some of us believed France makes the best Pinot Noir whereas others believed the best comes from California or Washington. That night, we were going to settle the score.

We chose one bottle from California, one bottle from Willamette Valley, Oregon, one bottle from Côte de Nuits, Bourgogne and one bottle from Irancy (also in Bourgogne but a small region in Chablis). In fact, it is the only region in Chablis permitted to produce Pinot Noir. (Fun fact)

The party's purpose was to blind taste the wines. The food we served took a backseat to the party's primary purpose. Yes, we had amazing food from an amazing chef at an amazing restaurant. But it was a restaurant and chef we all were familiar with; therefore, it did not take the lead from the tasting discussion or competition.

This is how I typically handle the opening of many of our pricier bottles. I revolve the occasion around the bottle as opposed to the bringing out the bottle for the occasion. The bottle of that magnitude should be the occasion.

I hope this helps your mentality when it comes to the nicer bottles in your collection. I am not saying, by any means, this is what you should do, but rather, this is how I, internally handle the decision. Agree or disagree?

Oh, in case you wondered.

1. Blooms Field – Domaine de la Côte– Santa Barbara County, California
2. Vosne-Romanée Premier Cru – Côte de Nuits, Bourgogne
3. Eyrie Vineyards – Willamette Valley, Oregon
4. Irancy – Chablis, Bourgogne

Fifteen
How I Make Wine:
How to not "screw it up"

When I started making wine over a decade ago, as I previously stated, it was not very good. In fact, it was atrocious. I would not serve it to my worst enemy, that's how bad it was. But I persevered and I did not stop. I watched video after video and studied book after book with the hope of understanding what made wine "good." Along the way, I garnered a few awards and earned a few certifications, but it all came down to study and perseverance.

I became one of the very first "Vayniacs." I followed Gary Vaynerchuck long before he was Gary Vee. Before he had Vaynermedia and well before he started VeeFriends or hosted VeeCon.

In fact, I still have his Thunder Red which, I believe, was his first vintage from 2005. I also have his first "sniffy sniff" wrist band that he sold to other Vayniacs via his YouTube channel through his wine club. Regardless of the value or importance of these items, the point is, I was early. Like, early. (Those in the Non Fungible Token (NFT) world understand)

In those days, there was no recipe to follow. I crushed wine, added yeast (store bought yeast), added sugar, and waited. Like I said, it was awful. Over the years and hundreds, if not thousands of dollars later, I got better. I truly believe I had to fail multiple times before was able to learn and improve from those failures. I believe this to be no different than learning the internet or NFTs. My first lesson in both costed me a few dollars to say the least.

Experimenting with wine is exactly that, experimenting. I enjoyed trying things knowing full well it would not turn out good. I needed that experience. I needed that knowledge. What happens if I do not oak Merlot? What happens if I oak Sauvignon Blanc? These things, though not routinely done needed tried. This is how I developed the understanding as to what each little variable did to the wine.

As my wine knowledge and I evolved, so did my winemaking process. I started to be specific about my yeast, my bottles, my sanitizer and even my water. If you do not believe the specific water should matter, try a glass of tap water and a glass of bottled water. It matters. (Or maybe it is just my Youngstown water)

At any rate, I became specific about my ingredients. This is essentially no different than my wife preferring fresh garlic from our garden as opposed to dried garlic from a jar when making her Sunday sauce.

As stated earlier, I cannot control another person's grapes or juice. I cannot control where the grapes were grown. I cannot control if they were grown next to a mint field which can give off a minty flavor to the Cabernet. But I can control a few other variables. So, I thought to myself, If I can control something, why don't I?

I can control the acid content which may make the Sauvignon crispier. I can control how long I leave the juice in oak which can make it taste more like "dirt" or possibly vanilla. I can control where my oak comes from. However, many variables I can control may improve the character, but if I make the wrong choice, I can also ruin a wine rather quickly.

My advice?

Do not screw it up.

Let nature do its thing.

For thousands of years, humans were making wine and it was probably just fine. The Romans and the Pope did not have fancy filtration systems. They did not have small bottles of flavor content to add chocolate or raspberry hints to the wine.

Nope – they had none of that

They had plain-old empty jugs and whole lot of patience. Centuries ago, our ancestors would literally bury the jug of smashed fruit in the ground and just wait. Eventually that juice would ferment, and eventually they would have wine. Why do we complicate the process so much? Why do we standardize the process?

So, when someone asks me "what do you do to your wine that makes it so good?" My typical answer is "I let nature do its thing and try not to screw it up." Though I have had my own fair share of screw ups, I wanted my readers to understand my process and what I did (for better or worse).

The following is the process in which I took to "not screw it up." It is, by no means, a recipe book on how to make the perfect wine. Let me be clear, the following is NOT how to make good wine but rather a copy of my winemaking diary over the past few years. Some decisions were good, and some were not so good. Either way, transparency is the key and here is what I did.

2019 – Concord

Step 1

Sanitize – Sanitize – Sanitize

- Buckets
- Air locks
- Spoons
- Tubing
- Hydrometer

Step 2

In a 6-gallon primary fermenter, add juice and top off with water. I use tap water – distilled water has no nutrients, and the yeast will need these.

Measure the specific gravity – you will need this number to calculate final alcohol content (1.08)

Add yeast nutrient and stir

I waited 24 hours to add yeast

Step 3

Add yeast on top

   Sprinkle – do not stir

   Airlock carboy

Step 4

After fermentation stopped, transfer to glass carboy leaving sediment behind

Place oak in carboy

Measure specific gravity (1.00)

Top off carboy – I used Old Vine Zinfandel this year as my blending agent

Step 5

Two weeks after oak was added, I siphoned the wine off the oak to a different carboy.

I then topped off again, but with water this time

Step 6

Stabilize the wine by mixing ¼ teaspoon potassium metabisulfite in ½ cup of water.

Let sit for a week

Step 7

Rack to another carboy and degas the wine

Step 8

Mix in clearing agent one week after it was degassed.

I used Super Kleer – Kieselsol and Chitosan combined

Step 9

One week after adding the clearing agent, mix potassium metabisulfite and sterilize the bottles and bucket.

Transfer wine to bucket for bottling (my bucket has a spicket which make bottling easy). Truly the only reason I resend to my bucket.

Step 10

Fill bottles – cork and allow to stand upright for 2 days before laying in a rack at an angle. This allows the cork to expand and seal the bottle.

2020 – Sauvignon Blanc
Awarded a Silver Medal in International Competition

Step 1

Sanitize – Sanitize – Sanitize

- Buckets
- Air locks
- Spoons
- Tubing
- Hydrometer

Step 2

In a 6-gallon primary fermenter, add juice and top off with warm water. I use tap water – distilled water has no nutrients that the yeast will need.

Measure the specific gravity – you will need this number to calculate final alcohol content (1.097)

Mix in Bentonite (done at the beginning with white wines)

Measured Acid level – 3.6

add yeast – sprinkle and do not stir

Step 3

After fermentation is done, rack to glass carboy

(After airlock stops bubbling)

Add potassium metabisulfite and potassium sorbate

Degas

Stir in Kieselsol

Step 4

Day after Kieselsol added, add Chitosan pack – stir

Top off with water or like wine (I used Torrontes to balance off the acid from the Sauvignon Blanc)

Step 5

Throughout the week, occasionally turn the carboy so sediment falls

Step 6

After 1 week of clearing, rack wine again to new carboy – I did this to get wine off the lies to NOT undergo malolactic fermentation

I topped off with Torrontes again.

Step 7

Two weeks after re-rack, I filtered the wine using a Buon Vino Mini Jet

I used a number 3 filter followed by a second round of filtration with a #1 filter (polishing pad).

Step 8

The day after filtration, I mixed potassium metabisulfite and sterilize the bottles and bucket.

Transfer wine to bucket for bottling (my bucket has a spicket which make bottling easy)

Step 9

Specific gravity at end – 0.994

Calculation for final alcohol content

Specific gravity at <u>start</u> minus specific gravity at <u>end</u> --- <u>then take this number and multiply by 131</u> (a number calculated by the density of ethanol)

So, for this wine our initial SG was 1.097

Our end SG was 0.994

So, 1.097 - 0.994 = 0.103

0.103 x 131 = 13.5%

2021 – Malbec
Awarded a Silver Medal in International Competition

Step 1

Sanitize – Sanitize – Sanitize

Buckets

Air locks

Spoons

Tubing

Hydrometer

Step 2

In a 6-gallon primary fermenter, add juice and top off with warm water. I use tap water – distilled water has no nutrients that the yeast will need.

Measure the specific gravity – you will need this number to calculate final alcohol content (1.097)

Mix in Bentonite

Oak pack recommended but I did not use (previous bad experience with these oak chips)

add yeast – sprinkle and do not stir

Step 3

After fermentation is done, rack to glass carboy to sit

Add potassium metabisulfite

Degas

Stir in Kieselsol

I added a small capful of Raspberry and Cherry flavoring

Step 4

The day after Kieselsol was added, I added Chitosan pack – stir

I did not top off at this point

Step 5

Throughout the week, occasionally turn the carboy so sediment falls

Step 6

After 1 week of clearing, rack wine again to new carboy

I topped off with Malbec

Step 7

Two weeks after re-rack, I filtered the wine using a Buon Vino Mini Jet

I used a number 2 filter and only filtered once for this wine.

Step 8

The day after filtration, I mixed potassium metabisulfite and sterilize the bottles and bucket.

I transferred wine to bucket for bottling (my bucket has a spicket which make bottling easy)

Step 9

Specific gravity at end – 0.990

Calculation

Specific gravity at start minus specific gravity at end --- then take this number and multiply by 131 (a number calculated by the density of ethanol)

So, for this wine our initial SG was 1.097

Our end SG was 0.990

So, 1.097 - 0.990 = 0.107

0.103 x 131 = 14%

Over the course of the past few years, I certainly have altered the recipe and the process. I have learned a lot and have manipulated a few things. I honestly feel that any "chef" finds his or her own way of doing things. For example, I prefer to transfer my wine back to my primary fermentation bucket because of the spicket on it that makes bottling so easy. I also find adding a small (very small) capful of natural flavoring adds a little something to my wines. Judges have commented on the "fruit" flavoring and have scored me well based on it. I certainly do not want it overpowering the wine, so a fraction of a cap is enough. We are not making fruit juice here. Or are we technically?

I also find it necessary to top off with wine as opposed to topping off with water. The first year I topped off with wine I used an agent to balance off the high acid Sauvignon Blanc whereas the Malbec year, I topped up with another Malbec. The reason I chose to top off with another Malbec was to capture some of their oak process since I did not add oak chips to my Malbec. I was hopeful by adding a similar wine when topping off I could capture some of the nuances in their oaking process.

Making wine is an experiment. I am, by no means, stating this is the perfect recipe. NOT EVEN CLOSE. I am saying, however, this is what I did, for better or for worse. I try to always be an open book, sometimes to a fault. Well, here is my open book. Please, learn from this and make your blend, your own.

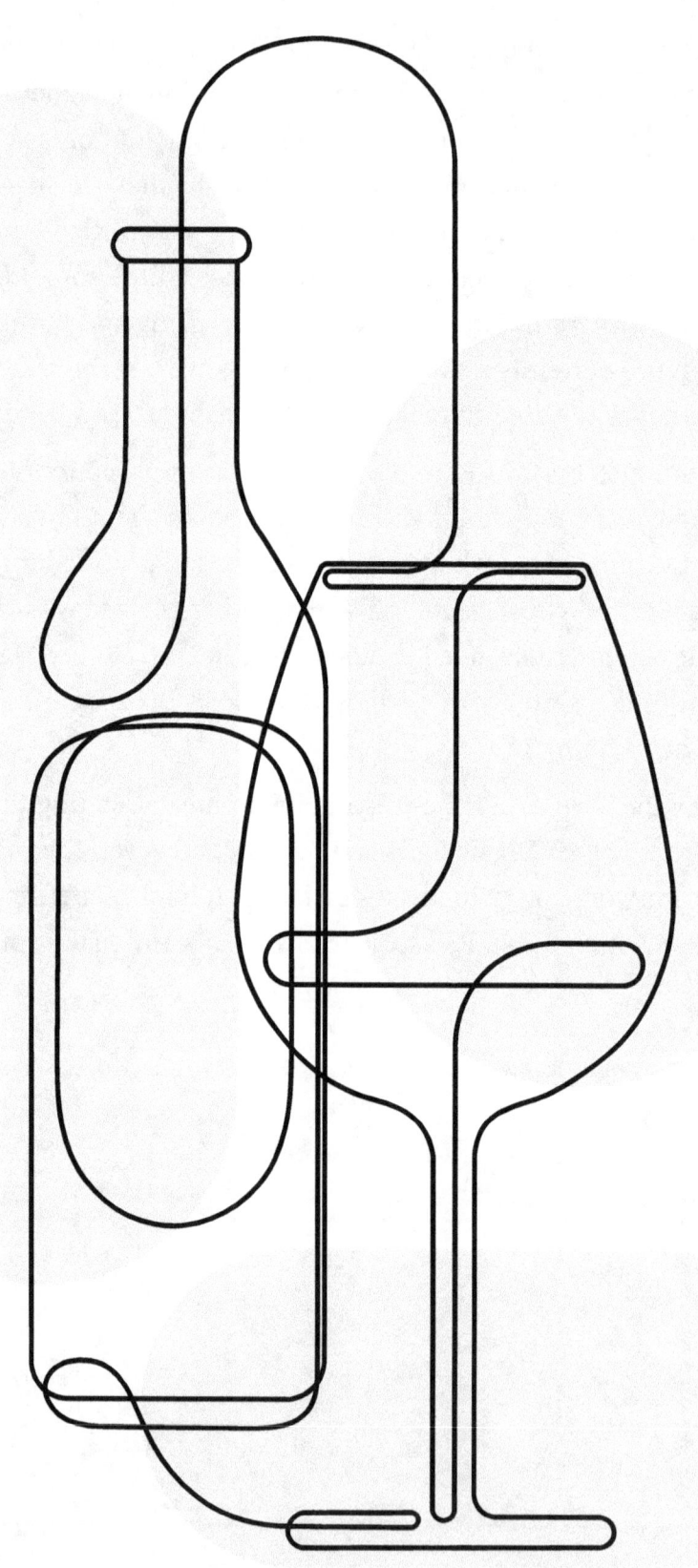

Conclusion

This book was designed and outlined to be a guide. I wanted my readers to get a glimpse into wine from the perspective of someone who never originally intended to be involved with wine. My career path led me into medicine and more specifically, into neurology.

I enjoy neurology but I also enjoy wine. I enjoy the collecting aspect as well as the making aspect of wine. I will taste the wine here and there but the collecting, studying, making, and educating about wine is where my true passion lies.

However, by far and away, my favorite thing to do with wine is intertwine how health and wine meet. That is why this book was so important to write. I wanted to give my readers a glimpse into my world with wine while also educating them on health. I wanted to dispel any rumors regarding migraines and wine while also discussing the French Paradox. I wanted my readers to understand how I got to where I am in the wine industry while also being transparent about my journey.

I am by no means an expert. Sure, I took a few classes and passed a few exams, but I know very little and continue to learn every day. Experts may read this book and scoff at some of my recommendations but again these are my recommendations for better or worse. Many winemakers may not like my process, but again this is how I did it, for better or worse.

I did not want this book to be the Bible on wine, but an enjoyable read in the hopes of my readers learn something. I appreciate wine and how to make it, but like any other chemical experiment, the process can and should change over time. Who wants cookie cutter wine? Certainly, not me.

I want this book to serve as a guide as you progress through the wine journey very similar to the way I progressed through the journey. Thank you for following along with me.

In the meantime, let me leave you with a few awesome facts.

"Party Knowledge" if you will -- (knowledge you can show off at a party)

Rule of Thumb

There are many theories as to where the phrase 'rule of thumb' originated. The one I prefer to believe is prior to thermometers, a winemaker would know when it was time to add yeast to his/her juice by testing it with their thumb. By sticking a person's thumb into the juice, a winemaker would rule that it is the right time to add yeast for fermentation to commence. Hence the phrase "rule of thumb."

To Your Health

When we are hosting a meal, we tend to raise our glasses and say, "To Your Health." There are multiple theories as to this phrase's origination. The two I find most interesting: During ancient times the host would raise his glass and state "to your health" to ensure to his guests that the wine they were about to consume was not poison. The other and less likely the real reason is that a Host would say this phrase to warn his guests that he may die from this drink and its spoilage so if he dies, here is to saving your health. AKA "To Your Health" and not mine.

Mind Your 'P's and 'Q's

Minding your 'P's and 'Q's originated from old Irish Pubs. Barkeeps would say this to the guests when they become unruly. In these pubs, patrons were known to order Pints and Quarts and when they became so intoxicated, the barkeep told them to "Mind their 'P's and 'Q's."

Honeymoon

As explained before, many of us know the word "honeymoon" to be associated with a wedding and the vacation a newly married couple takes typically shortly after they say their I Dos. But that is not what the term "honeymoon's" original intent. It was customary for the father of the bride to ferment enough Honey Mead to last the newly married couple from one full moon to the next full moon. Hence the term "Honeymoon."

Appendix A - 2020 Wine Competition - P-01

2020 WineMaker International Amateur WINE COMPETITION

Flight: 298

Entry: 981

Category: Red Native American Varietal (Concord)

Awarded Points

Appearance (maximum 3 points)

☑ Excellent – Brilliant with outstanding characteristic color (3 points)
☐ Good – Clear with characteristic color (2 points)
☐ Needs Improvement – Slight haze and/or slight off color (1 point)
☐ Objectionable – Cloudy and/or off color (0 points)

Comments _nice color extraction_

3

Aroma and Bouquet (maximum 6 points)

☐ Exceptional – Wonderful characteristic aroma of grape variety or wine type. Outstanding and complex bouquet. Exceptional balance of aroma and bouquet. (6 points)
☐ Excellent – Strong characteristic aroma of grape variety or wine type. Complex bouquet. Good balance of aroma and bouquet. (5 points)
☐ Good – Good characteristic aroma of grape variety or wine type. Admirable bouquet. (4 points)
☐ Pleasant – Good characteristic aroma of grape variety or wine type. Pleasant bouquet. (3 points)
☐ Acceptable – No perceptible aroma or bouquet or with slight off odors (2 points)
☐ Needs Improvement – Off odors very detectable (1 point)
☐ Objectionable – Offensive odors (0 points)

Comments _getting a chemical solvent_

2.5

Taste (maximum 6 points)

☐ Exceptional – Wonderful characteristic flavor of grape variety or wine type. Outstanding balance. Smooth, full-bodied and outstanding. (6 points)
☐ Excellent – Strong characteristic flavor of grape variety or wine type. Excellent balance and body, but not quite outstanding. (5 points)
☐ Good – Good characteristic flavor of grape variety or wine type. Good balance. May have some minor imperfections. (4 points)
☑ Pleasant – Pleasant flavor of grape variety or wine type. May be slightly out of balance and/or have minor off flavors. (3 points)
☐ Acceptable – A hint of flavor of grape variety or wine type. Detectable out of balance flavors with more pronounced faults than above. (2 points)
☐ Needs Improvement – Disagreeable off flavors and a poor balance. (1 point)
☐ Objectionable – Offensive flavors (0 points)

Comments _have an well dialed tandard_
concord flavor a wee bit high

2.5

Aftertaste (maximum 3 points)

☐ Excellent – Lingering outstanding aftertaste (3 points)
☐ Good – Pleasant aftertaste (2 points)
☑ Needs Improvement – Little or no distinguishable aftertaste (1 point)
☐ Objectionable – Unpleasant aftertaste (0 points)

Comments _____

2

Overall Impression (maximum 2 points)

☐ Excellent (2 points)
☐ Good (1 point)
☐ Objectionable (0 points)

Comments _____

1

Judge Signature _____

Verification _____

Judge # 32

Total Points Awarded 11

Flight: 298   **Entry: 981**

Appendix A - 2020 Wine Competition - P-02

2020 WineMaker International Amateur WINE COMPETITION

Entry: 981

Flight: 298

Category: Red Native American Varietal (Concord)

Awarded Points

Appearance (maximum 3 points)

☐ Excellent – Brilliant with outstanding characteristic color (3 points)
☐ Good – Clear with characteristic color (2 points)
☐ Needs Improvement – Slight haze and/or slight off color (1 point)
☐ Objectionable – Cloudy and/or off color (0 points)

Comments

Aroma and Bouquet (maximum 6 points)

☐ Exceptional – Wonderful characteristic aroma of grape variety or wine type. Outstanding and complex bouquet. Exceptional balance of aroma and bouquet. (6 points)
☐ Excellent – Strong characteristic aroma of grape variety or wine type. Complex bouquet. Good balance of aroma and bouquet. (5 points)
☐ Good – Good characteristic aroma of grape variety or wine type. Admirable bouquet. (4 points)
☐ Pleasant – Good characteristic aroma of grape variety or wine type. Pleasant bouquet. (3 points)
☐ Acceptable – No perceptible aroma or bouquet or with slight off odors (2 points)
☐ Needs Improvement – Off odors very detectable (1 point)
☐ Objectionable – Offensive odors (0 points)

Comments

Taste (maximum 6 points)

☐ Exceptional – Wonderful characteristic flavor of grape variety or wine type. Outstanding balance. Smooth, full-bodied and outstanding. (6 points)
☐ Excellent – Strong characteristic flavor of grape variety or wine type. Excellent balance and body, but not quite outstanding. (5 points)
☐ Good – Good characteristic flavor of grape variety or wine type. Good balance. May have some minor imperfections. (4 points)
☐ Pleasant – Pleasant flavor of grape variety or wine type. May be slightly out of balance and/or have minor off flavors. (3 points)
☐ Acceptable – A hint of flavor of grape variety or wine type. Detectable out of balance flavors with more pronounced faults than above. (2 points)
☐ Needs Improvement – Disagreeable off flavors and a poor balance. (1 point)
☐ Objectionable – Offensive flavors (0 points)

Comments

Aftertaste (maximum 3 points)

☐ Excellent – Lingering outstanding aftertaste (3 points)
☐ Good – Pleasant aftertaste (2 points)
☐ Needs Improvement – Little or no distinguishable aftertaste (1 point)
☐ Objectionable – Unpleasant aftertaste (0 points)

Comments

Overall Impression (maximum 2 points)

☐ Excellent (2 points)
☐ Good (1 point)
☐ Objectionable (0 points)

Comments

Judge Signature

Verification

Judge #_____

Flight: 298   Entry: 981

Total Points Awarded

Appendix A - 2020 Wine Competition - P-03

2020 WineMaker International Amateur WINE COMPETITION

Flight: 298

Entry: 981

Category: Red Native American Varietal (Concord)

Awarded Points

Appearance (maximum 3 points)

☑ Excellent – Brilliant with outstanding characteristic color (3 points)
☐ Good – Clear with characteristic color (2 points)
☐ Needs Improvement – Slight haze and/or slight off color (1 point)
☐ Objectionable – Cloudy and/or off color (0 points)

Comments _____

Aroma and Bouquet (maximum 6 points)

☐ Exceptional – Wonderful characteristic aroma of grape variety or wine type. Outstanding and complex bouquet. Exceptional balance of aroma and bouquet. (6 points)
☐ Excellent – Strong characteristic aroma of grape variety or wine type. Complex bouquet. Good balance of aroma and bouquet. (5 points)
☐ Good – Good characteristic aroma of grape variety or wine type. Admirable bouquet. (4 points)
☐ Pleasant – Good characteristic aroma of grape variety or wine type. Pleasant bouquet. (3 points)
☑ Acceptable – No perceptible aroma or bouquet or with slight off odors (2 points)
☐ Needs Improvement – Off odors very detectable (1 point)
☐ Objectionable – Offensive odors (0 points)

Comments _____

Taste (maximum 6 points)

☐ Exceptional – Wonderful characteristic flavor of grape variety or wine type. Outstanding balance. Smooth, full-bodied and outstanding. (6 points)
☐ Excellent – Strong characteristic flavor of grape variety or wine type. Excellent balance and body, but not quite outstanding. (5 points)
☐ Good – Good characteristic flavor of grape variety or wine type. Good balance. May have some minor imperfections. (4 points)
☐ Pleasant – Pleasant flavor of grape variety or wine type. May be slightly out of balance and/or have minor off flavors. (3 points)
☑ Acceptable – A hint of flavor of grape variety or wine type. Detectable out of balance flavors with more pronounced faults than above. (2 points)
☐ Needs Improvement – Disagreeable off flavors and a poor balance. (1 point)
☐ Objectionable – Offensive flavors (0 points)

Comments _____

Aftertaste (maximum 3 points)

☐ Excellent – Lingering outstanding aftertaste (3 points)
☐ Good – Pleasant aftertaste (2 points)
☑ Needs Improvement – Little or no distinguishable aftertaste (1 point)
☐ Objectionable – Unpleasant aftertaste (0 points)

Comments _____

Overall Impression (maximum 2 points)

☐ Excellent (2 points)
☑ Good (1 point)
☐ Objectionable (0 points)

Comments _____

Judge Signature _____

Verification _____

Judge # 33

Flight: 298   **Entry: 981**   **Total Points Awarded**

Appendix B - 2021 Wine Competition - P-01

2021 WineMaker International Amateur WINE COMPETITION

Entry: 120

Category: Sauvignon Blanc

Flight: 238

Awarded Points

Appearance (maximum 3 points)

☐ Excellent – Brilliant with outstanding characteristic color (3 points)
☐ Good – Clear with characteristic color (2 points)
☐ Needs Improvement – Slight haze and/or slight off color (1 point)
☐ Objectionable – Cloudy and/or off color (0 points)

Comments _Light Clear, Lemon Yellow_

3

Aroma and Bouquet (maximum 6 points)

☐ Exceptional – Wonderful characteristic aroma of grape variety or wine type. Outstanding and complex bouquet. Exceptional balance of aroma and bouquet. (6 points)
☐ Excellent – Strong characteristic aroma of grape variety or wine type. Complex bouquet. Good balance of aroma and bouquet. (5 points)
☐ Good – Good characteristic aroma of grape variety or wine type. Admirable bouquet. (4 points)
☐ Pleasant – Good characteristic aroma of grape variety or wine type. Pleasant bouquet. (3 points)
☐ Acceptable – No perceptible aroma or bouquet or with slight off odors (2 points)
☐ Needs Improvement – Off odors very detectable (1 point)
☐ Objectionable – Offensive odors (0 points)

Comments _Citrus, Lemon Lime_ SO_2

4

Taste (maximum 6 points)

☐ Exceptional – Wonderful characteristic flavor of grape variety or wine type. Outstanding balance. Smooth, full-bodied and outstanding. (6 points)
☐ Excellent – Strong characteristic flavor of grape variety or wine type. Excellent balance and body, but not quite outstanding. (5 points)
☐ Good – Good characteristic flavor of grape variety or wine type. Good balance. May have some minor imperfections. (4 points)
☐ Pleasant – Pleasant flavor of grape variety or wine type. May be slightly out of balance and/or have minor off flavors. (3 points)
☐ Acceptable – A hint of flavor of grape variety or wine type. Detectable out of balance flavors with more pronounced faults than above. (2 points)
☐ Needs Improvement – Disagreeable off flavors and a poor balance. (1 point)
☐ Objectionable – Offensive flavors (0 points)

Comments _SO_2 Citrus, Lemon + Lime_

4

Aftertaste (maximum 3 points)

☐ Excellent – Lingering outstanding aftertaste (3 points)
☐ Good – Pleasant aftertaste (2 points)
☐ Needs Improvement – Little or no distinguishable aftertaste (1 point)
☐ Objectionable – Unpleasant aftertaste (0 points)

Comments _Flavors Linger – SO_2 not blown off_

2

Overall Impression (maximum 2 points)

☐ Excellent (2 points)
☐ Good (1 point)
☐ Objectionable (0 points)

Comments _Nice_

1

Judge Signature _Mark_

Verification _CC_

Judge # _4_

14

Total Points Awarded

Flight: 238   **Entry: 120**

Appendix B - 2021 Wine Competition - P-02

2021 WineMaker International Amateur WINE COMPETITION

Flight: 238

Entry: 120

Category: Sauvignon Blanc

Awarded Points

Appearance (maximum 3 points)

☐ Excellent – Brilliant with outstanding characteristic color (3 points)
☐ Good – Clear with characteristic color (2 points)
☐ Needs Improvement – Slight haze and/or slight off color (1 point)
☐ Objectionable – Cloudy and/or off color (0 points)

Comments

2.5

Aroma and Bouquet (maximum 6 points)

☐ Exceptional – Wonderful characteristic aroma of grape variety or wine type. Outstanding and complex bouquet. Exceptional balance of aroma and bouquet. (6 points)
☐ Excellent – Strong characteristic aroma of grape variety or wine type. Complex bouquet. Good balance of aroma and bouquet. (5 points)
☐ Good – Good characteristic aroma of grape variety or wine type. Admirable bouquet. (4 points)
☐ Pleasant – Good characteristic aroma of grape variety or wine type. Pleasant bouquet. (3 points)
☐ Acceptable – No perceptible aroma or bouquet or with slight off odors (2 points)
☐ Needs Improvement – Off odors very detectable (1 point)
☐ Objectionable – Offensive odors (0 points)

Comments LIGHT, CLEAN NOT VARIETAL

3

Taste (maximum 6 points)

☐ Exceptional – Wonderful characteristic flavor of grape variety or wine type. Outstanding balance. Smooth, full-bodied and outstanding. (6 points)
☐ Excellent – Strong characteristic flavor of grape variety or wine type. Excellent balance and body, but not quite outstanding. (5 points)
☐ Good – Good characteristic flavor of grape variety or wine type. Good balance. May have some minor imperfections. (4 points)
☐ Pleasant – Pleasant flavor of grape variety or wine type. May be slightly out of balance and/or have minor off flavors. (3 points)
☐ Acceptable – A hint of flavor of grape variety or wine type. Detectable out of balance flavors with more pronounced faults than above. (2 points)
☐ Needs Improvement – Disagreeable off flavors and a poor balance. (1 point)
☐ Objectionable – Offensive flavors (0 points)

Comments GOOD BALANCE, SIMPLE WINE

3.

Aftertaste (maximum 3 points)

☐ Excellent – Lingering outstanding aftertaste (3 points)
☐ Good – Pleasant aftertaste (2 points)
☐ Needs Improvement – Little or no distinguishable aftertaste (1 point)
☐ Objectionable – Unpleasant aftertaste (0 points)

Comments SHORT FINISH

1.5

Overall Impression (maximum 2 points)

☐ Excellent (2 points)
☐ Good (1 point)
☐ Objectionable (0 points)

Comments

1.

Judge Signature

Verification C.V

Judge # 25

11.

Total Points Awarded

Flight: 238   Entry: 120

Appendix B - 2021 Wine Competition - P-03

2021 WineMaker International Amateur WINE COMPETITION

Entry: 120

Category: Sauvignon Blanc

Flight: 238

Awarded Points

Appearance (maximum 3 points)

☑ Excellent – Brilliant with outstanding characteristic color (3 points)
☐ Good – Clear with characteristic color (2 points)
☐ Needs Improvement – Slight haze and/or slight off color (1 point)
☐ Objectionable – Cloudy and/or off color (0 points)

Comments _____

3.0

Aroma and Bouquet (maximum 6 points)

☐ Exceptional – Wonderful characteristic aroma of grape variety or wine type. Outstanding and complex bouquet. Exceptional balance of aroma and bouquet. (6 points)
☐ Excellent – Strong characteristic aroma of grape variety or wine type. Complex bouquet. Good balance of aroma and bouquet. (5 points)
☑ Good – Good characteristic aroma of grape variety or wine type. Admirable bouquet. (4 points)
☐ Pleasant – Good characteristic aroma of grape variety or wine type. Pleasant bouquet. (3 points)
☐ Acceptable – No perceptible aroma or bouquet or with slight off odors (2 points)
☐ Needs Improvement – Off odors very detectable (1 point)
☐ Objectionable – Offensive odors (0 points)

Comments _____

4.5

Taste (maximum 6 points)

☐ Exceptional – Wonderful characteristic flavor of grape variety or wine type. Outstanding balance. Smooth, full-bodied and outstanding. (6 points)
☐ Excellent – Strong characteristic flavor of grape variety or wine type. Excellent balance and body, but not quite outstanding. (5 points)
☑ Good – Good characteristic flavor of grape variety or wine type. Good balance. May have some minor imperfections. (4 points)
☐ Pleasant – Pleasant flavor of grape variety or wine type. May be slightly out of balance and/or have minor off flavors. (3 points)
☐ Acceptable – A hint of flavor of grape variety or wine type. Detectable out of balance flavors with more pronounced faults than above. (2 points)
☐ Needs Improvement – Disagreeable off flavors and a poor balance. (1 point)
☐ Objectionable – Offensive flavors (0 points)

Comments _____

4.0

Aftertaste (maximum 3 points)

☐ Excellent – Lingering outstanding aftertaste (3 points)
☐ Good – Pleasant aftertaste (2 points)
☐ Needs Improvement – Little or no distinguishable aftertaste (1 point)
☐ Objectionable – Unpleasant aftertaste (0 points)

Comments _____

2.0

Overall impression (maximum 2 points)

☐ Excellent (2 points)
☐ Good (1 point)
☐ Objectionable (0 points)

Comments _____

1.5

Judge Signature _____

Verification _____

Judge # _22_

15.0

Total Points Awarded

Flight: 238   Entry: 120

Appendix C - 2021 Award

Appendix D - 2022 Wine Competition - P-01

2022 WineMaker International Amateur WINE COMPETITION

Entry: 151

Flight: 109

Category: Other Red Vinifera Varietals (Malbec)

	Awarded Points

Appearance (maximum 3 points)

- ☐ Excellent – Brilliant with outstanding characteristic color (3 points)
- ☐ Good – Clear with characteristic color (2 points)
- ☐ Needs Improvement – Slight haze and/or slight off color (1 point)
- ☐ Objectionable – Cloudy and/or off color (0 points)

Comments _____ Good Garnet

3.0

Aroma and Bouquet (maximum 6 points)

- ☐ Exceptional – Wonderful characteristic aroma of grape variety or wine type. Outstanding and complex bouquet. Exceptional balance of aroma and bouquet. (6 points)
- ☐ Excellent – Strong characteristic aroma of grape variety or wine type. Complex bouquet. Good balance of aroma and bouquet. (5 points)
- ☐ Good – Good characteristic aroma of grape variety or wine type. Admirable bouquet. (4 points)
- ☐ Pleasant – Good characteristic aroma of grape variety or wine type. Pleasant bouquet. (3 points)
- ☐ Acceptable – No perceptible aroma or bouquet or with slight off odors (2 points)
- ☐ Needs Improvement – Off odors very detectable (1 point)
- ☐ Objectionable – Offensive odors (0 points)

Comments _____ Good Red Fruit

4.5

Taste (maximum 6 points)

- ☐ Exceptional – Wonderful characteristic flavor of grape variety or wine type. Outstanding balance. Smooth, full-bodied and outstanding. (6 points)
- ☐ Excellent – Strong characteristic flavor of grape variety or wine type. Excellent balance and body, but not quite outstanding. (5 points)
- ☐ Good – Good characteristic flavor of grape variety or wine type. Good balance. May have some minor imperfections. (4 points)
- ☐ Pleasant – Pleasant flavor of grape variety or wine type. May be slightly out of balance and/or have minor off flavors. (3 points)
- ☐ Acceptable – A hint of flavor of grape variety or wine type. Detectable out of balance flavors with more pronounced faults than above. (2 points)
- ☐ Needs Improvement – Disagreeable off flavors and a poor balance. (1 point)
- ☐ Objectionable – Offensive flavors (0 points)

Comments _____ Good Red Fruit, well balanced.

4.0

Aftertaste (maximum 3 points)

- ☐ Excellent – Lingering outstanding aftertaste (3 points)
- ☐ Good – Pleasant aftertaste (2 points)
- ☐ Needs Improvement – Little or no distinguishable aftertaste (1 point)
- ☐ Objectionable – Unpleasant aftertaste (0 points)

Comments _____ Med Finish — Good Fruit ATA.

1.5

Overall Impression (maximum 2 points)

- ☐ Excellent (2 points)
- ☐ Good (1 point)
- ☐ Objectionable (0 points)

Comments _____ Nice Tannins

1.0

Judge # **23**

Judge Signature _____

Verification _____

14.0

Total Points Awarded

Flight: 109   Entry: 151

Appendix D - 2022 Wine Competition - P-02

2022 WineMaker International Amateur WINE COMPETITION

Flight: 109

Entry: 151

Category: Other Red Vinifera Varietals (Malbec)

Awarded Points

Appearance (maximum 3 points)

☐ Excellent – Brilliant with outstanding characteristic color (3 points)
☐ Good – Clear with characteristic color (2 points)
☐ Needs Improvement – Slight haze and/or slight off color (1 point)
☐ Objectionable – Cloudy and/or off color (0 points)

Comments _____ Good clarity

2

Aroma and Bouquet (maximum 6 points)

☐ Exceptional – Wonderful characteristic aroma of grape variety or wine type. Outstanding and complex bouquet. Exceptional balance of aroma and bouquet. (6 points)
☐ Excellent – Strong characteristic aroma of grape variety or wine type. Complex bouquet. Good balance of aroma and bouquet. (5 points)
☐ Good – Good characteristic aroma of grape variety or wine type. Admirable bouquet. (4 points)
☐ Pleasant – Good characteristic aroma of grape variety or wine type. Pleasant bouquet. (3 points)
☐ Acceptable – No perceptible aroma or bouquet or with slight off odors (2 points)
☐ Needs Improvement – Off odors very detectable (1 point)
☐ Objectionable – Offensive odors (0 points)

Comments _____

3.5

Taste (maximum 6 points)

☐ Exceptional – Wonderful characteristic flavor of grape variety or wine type. Outstanding balance. Smooth, full-bodied and outstanding. (6 points)
☐ Excellent – Strong characteristic flavor of grape variety or wine type. Excellent balance and body, but not quite outstanding. (5 points)
☐ Good – Good characteristic flavor of grape variety or wine type. Good balance. May have some minor imperfections. (4 points)
☐ Pleasant – Pleasant flavor of grape variety or wine type. May be slightly out of balance and/or have minor off flavors. (3 points)
☐ Acceptable – A hint of flavor of grape variety or wine type. Detectable out of balance flavors with more pronounced faults than above. (2 points)
☐ Needs Improvement – Disagreeable off flavors and a poor balance. (1 point)
☐ Objectionable – Offensive flavors (0 points)

Comments _____ Good balance. If wine fresh grape needs a little more time under extraction to pull even more fruit.

4

Aftertaste (maximum 3 points)

☐ Excellent – Lingering outstanding aftertaste (3 points)
☐ Good – Pleasant aftertaste (2 points)
☐ Needs Improvement – Little or no distinguishable aftertaste (1 point)
☐ Objectionable – Unpleasant aftertaste (0 points)

Comments _____

2

Overall Impression (maximum 2 points)

☐ Excellent (2 points)
☐ Good (1 point)
☐ Objectionable (0 points)

Comments _____ Nice job!

1

Judge Signature _____

Verification _____

Judge # 25

12.5

Total Points Awarded

Flight: 109   **Entry: 151**

Appendix D - 2022 Wine Competition - P-03

2022 WineMaker International Amateur WINE COMPETITION

Entry: 151

Flight: 109

Category: Other Red Vinifera Varietals (Malbec)

Awarded Points

Appearance (maximum 3 points)

☐ Excellent – Brilliant with outstanding characteristic color (3 points)
☐ Good – Clear with characteristic color (2 points)
☐ Needs Improvement – Slight haze and/or slight off color (1 point)
☐ Objectionable – Cloudy and/or off color (0 points)

Comments _Reddish Black - Full to Rim_

3

Aroma and Bouquet (maximum 6 points)

☐ Exceptional – Wonderful characteristic aroma of grape variety or wine type. Outstanding and complex bouquet. Exceptional balance of aroma and bouquet. (6 points)
☐ Excellent – Strong characteristic aroma of grape variety or wine type. Complex bouquet. Good balance of aroma and bouquet. (5 points)
☐ Good – Good characteristic aroma of grape variety or wine type. Admirable bouquet. (4 points)
☐ Pleasant – Good characteristic aroma of grape variety or wine type. Pleasant bouquet. (3 points)
☐ Acceptable – No perceptible aroma or bouquet or with slight off odors (2 points)
☐ Needs Improvement – Off odors very detectable (1 point)
☐ Objectionable – Offensive odors (0 points)

Comments _Fruit - plums + cherries_

3

Taste (maximum 6 points)

☐ Exceptional – Wonderful characteristic flavor of grape variety or wine type. Outstanding balance. Smooth, full-bodied and outstanding. (6 points)
☐ Excellent – Strong characteristic flavor of grape variety or wine type. Excellent balance and body, but not quite outstanding. (5 points)
☐ Good – Good characteristic flavor of grape variety or wine type. Good balance. May have some minor imperfections. (4 points)
☐ Pleasant – Pleasant flavor of grape variety or wine type. May be slightly out of balance and/or have minor off flavors. (3 points)
☐ Acceptable – A hint of flavor of grape variety or wine type. Detectable out of balance flavors with more pronounced faults than above. (2 points)
☐ Needs Improvement – Disagreeable off flavors and a poor balance. (1 point)
☐ Objectionable – Offensive flavors (0 points)

Comments _Jammy - fruity - oak_

4

Aftertaste (maximum 3 points)

☐ Excellent – Lingering outstanding aftertaste (3 points)
☐ Good – Pleasant aftertaste (2 points)
☐ Needs Improvement – Little or no distinguishable aftertaste (1 point)
☐ Objectionable – Unpleasant aftertaste (0 points)

Comments _Unfinished_

2

Overall Impression (maximum 2 points)

☐ Excellent (2 points)
☐ Good (1 point)
☐ Objectionable (0 points)

Comments _Interesting_

1

Judge Signature _____

Verification _____

Judge # _24_

13

Total Points Awarded

Appendix E - 2022 Award

Be sure to follow us on
Twitter - @vannysvineyards

Check out our website
www.vannysvineyards.com

Shop our merchandise
https://www.bonfire.com/store/vannys-vineyards/

Drop us a comment
vannysvineyards@gmail.com